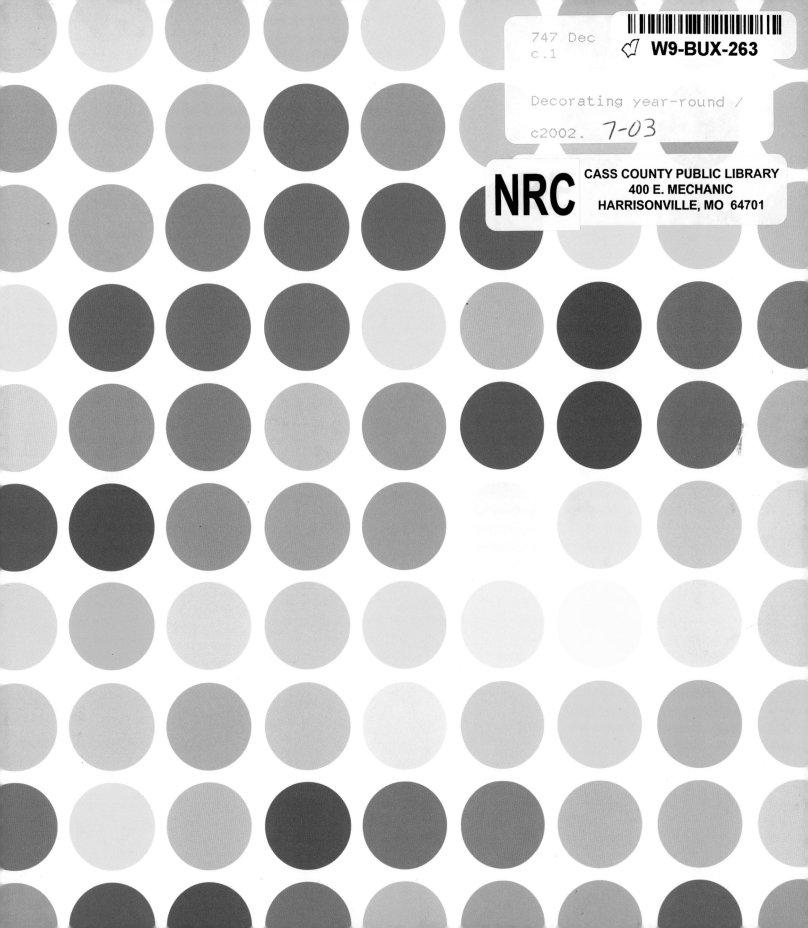

Better Homes and Gardens®
decorating
year-round

Better Homes and Gardens® Books
Des Moines, Iowa

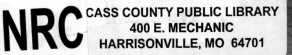

Better Homes and Gardens® Books
An imprint of Meredith® Books

Decorating Year-Round
Editor: Vicki L. Ingham
Contributing Editor: Rebecca Jerdee
Contributing Art Director: Sundie Ruppert
Copy Chief: Terri Fredrickson
Copy and Production Editor: Victoria Forlini
Editorial Operations Manager: Karen Schirm
Managers, Book Production: Pam Kvitne, Marjorie J. Schenkelberg
Contributing Copy Editor: Carol Boker
Contributing Proofreaders: Beth Lastine, Nancy Ruhling, Sherri Schultz
Indexer: Beverley Nightenhelser
Electronic Production Coordinator: Paula Forest
Editorial and Design Assistants: Kaye Chabot, Mary Lee Gavin

Meredith® Books
Editor in Chief: James D. Blume
Design Director: Matt Strelecki
Managing Editor: Gregory H. Kayko
Executive Editor, Home Decorating and Design: Denise L. Caringer

Director, Sales, Special Markets: Rita McMullen
Director, Sales, Premiums: Michael A. Peterson
Director, Sales, Retail: Tom Wierzbicki
Director, Book Marketing: Brad Elmitt
Director, Operations: George A. Susral
Director, Production: Douglas M. Johnston

Vice President and General Manager: Douglas J. Guendel

Better Homes and Gardens® Magazine
Editor in Chief: Karol DeWulf Nickell
Executive Building Editor: Joan McCloskey
Executive Interior Design Editor: Sandra S. Soria

Meredith Publishing Group
President, Publishing Group: Stephen M. Lacy
Vice President-Publishing Director: Bob Mate

Meredith Corporation
Chairman and Chief Executive Officer: William T. Kerr

Chairman of the Executive Committee: E. T. Meredith III

All of us at Better Homes and Gardens® Books are dedicated to providing you with information and ideas to enhance your home. We welcome your comments and suggestions. Write to us at: Better Homes and Gardens Books, Home Decorating and Design Editorial Department, 1716 Locust St., Des Moines, IA 50309-3023.

If you would like to purchase any of our home decorating and design, cooking, crafts, gardening, or home improvement books, check wherever quality books are sold. Or visit us at: bhgbooks.com

Cover Photographs: Kim Cornelison, Jon Jensen

table of contents

introduction

Little things mean a lot. In the spirited world of seasonal decorating, small changes have the power to alter a mood, freshen a room, or put a whole new face on the same old place. This book is about the little things—the small, bright changes you can make to spark up what you already have and breathe new life into rooms that have grown stale over time.

For example, this entry shows you how little decorative ideas can alter a space just inside the door. While the walls and furniture pieces remain the same, accessories and furniture placements don't. For a quick trip through a decorating year, compare this springtime scene to the summer, autumn, and winter versions on the following pages.

spring

summer

Playing off warm peach walls, summer-white accessories bring a fresh simplicity to the entry. White chandelier shades, large specimen seashells, a white platter on an easel, and a new cover for the pillow on the hall chair add up to sparkling, clean changes. A slim, white machine-washable cotton runner replaces the spring-green sisal rug on the floor, and green plants go outdoors for sunshine and rain.

Note the changes in the large glass urn beside the chair. For spring, it works as a vase, showing off a cavalcade of bright flower arrangements. In summer, it becomes a dry aquarium that sits idle for the season. To make the aquarium, simply sift three colors of sand in layers in the bottom of an urn. Top off the sand with a specimen starfish that symbolizes the season of beaches and fun in the sun.

The season of harvest suggests color and abundance for decorating. Pumpkin colors work well with these warm-colored walls, making them appear more intense than they did in spring. A new pillow cover and warm-color candles replace white accessories, and green plants return from their months outdoors. Underfoot, a large, patterned area rug offers a more substantial surface for the entry during the cool seasons.

The glass urn changes from a dry aquarium to a potpourri container. Tiny dried lemons and oranges, clove balls, miniature corn, nuts, and spices scent the air with fall's curious and delicious riches.

autumn

winter

Once fall colors pass into dormancy, white returns in its wintry form. Softer than the bright whites of summer, winter whites come in a variety of pale colors. Cobbled together with evergreens and bits of bright red, winter's decorating promises rest and a safe, secure return to spring.

Light winter with candles for warmth, add snuggly wraps for protection, and celebrate the dormant season with symbols of returning spring. Here, the chandelier is draped with greenery, and the chair welcomes a throw. The urn becomes a candleholder, and ornaments fill glass containers.

For a wealth of seasonal decorating ideas, please turn the pages of this book. You'll find some projects you can do by just looking at the pictures and others that will take more time to accomplish.

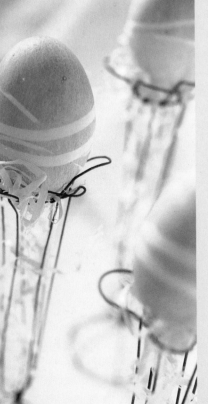

You know it well: the heady vertigo brought on by purple cro-cuses stretching upward through the snow. While tulips unfurl and daffodils crane their necks toward the sun, you emerge from winter's cocoon to open windows and air out rooms. In the intoxicating spin of spring fever, the world of home expands and you're suddenly free to decorate a larger world.

spring

color it fresh

Spring's mild color palette has a tender, reassuring personality quite different from the other three seasons. While summer's colors vibrate with intensity, fall's colors enrich, and winter's colors stand in stark contrast to each other, spring's gentle pastels combine to create a sweet and luscious atmosphere. You'll recognize spring's palette in the fragrant blooms of hyacinths and lilacs; in the soft, creamy, smooth-as-butter yellows of corn silk; and in the pale light greens of newborn shoots of grass. If you love color but can't live with strong ones, this delicate palette may fit your decorating personality. Here's a home that illustrates spring's light and airy style.

Classic white furniture, walls, and carpet provide a quiet, unchanging backdrop for a constantly changing array of decorative objects. From mantel to coffee table and from room to room, ironstone and wood finials move about the house as entertainment for the adoring eye. Their shapes are appreciated because the white backdrop never interferes or competes for attention.

Sugar pink is springtime sweet and pure, soft, and loving, but if it takes over a room, it can provide too much candy for the eye. For a pastel color scheme, combine small amounts of gently stimulating pinks and lavenders with large quantities of white to keep oversweetness and sugary effects at bay. Add pale greens and blues for balance; they'll cool affectionate tones with their naturally refreshing and comforting qualities.

Pretty-in-pink pieces of 1880s English luster dishes, *opposite,* delight the eye that loves pink in its various shades. Myriad patterns live together harmoniously, thanks to the color link. The white backdrop of the cupboard keeps the collection in good company.

The white-painted dining room, *right,* offering views of the river below, is the perfect theatrical backdrop for observing a panorama of seasons and the subtle changes created by the movement of the sun throughout the day.

For privacy's sake, plain white folding shutters frame the bedroom windows, *left,* that are usually kept open for enjoying beautiful views. The poster bed, with its architectural frame, is free of bed curtains for the sake of the same, unimpeded view.

Showcase special objects of desire against plain white walls as if they were sculptures in a gallery of art. Small shots of springtime colors are sweet relief in an all-white room, *opposite,* and in spite of their small size, they add a big-impact focal point to the space. The tiny jewelry chest and an antique mirror take center stage.

Spring's color personality looks at life through rose-colored glasses, with an optimistic attitude that teaches an appreciation of subtle surfaces, simple things, and objects close to the heart. It looks outward through the windows of the house with an eye that values ever-changing seasonal views as if they were paintings on a wall. To assure yourself of such enjoyments, keep windows and bed frames unadorned by cumbersome, patterned fabrics, and fill the room with furniture pieces that provide a foundation for living simply. Against this plain backdrop, show off precious pieces that tell personal stories and describe your travels.

Antiques At Home

junk style

To give your rooms a spring attitude, look toward the fragrant world at large. Garden if you have the space, and learn about color from flowers. Live comfortably with your sentimental choices, sink into casual furniture pieces that have relaxed airs, and give yourself plenty of display space to show off and enjoy your favorite decorative objects.

Settle into generous floral-patterned pillows and cushions, *opposite*. Hang garden trellises, scatter antique watering cans on tabletops, and feed the birds and animals. If sunlight and pets destroy fabric coverings, plan to replace them every three years. It will become your opportunity to experience a different set of floral prints.

Sometimes a chair isn't a chair. It might be a table, *above,* handy for displaying an artful arrangement of garden roses and tiny collectible colored-glass bottles.

wake up a corner

Throw open the
windows, breathe in the
air, and stretch your
decorating muscles—
the exercise will do you
good. While outdoor
flowers break through
winter's trail of dirt and
grime, freshen indoor
spaces with blooms on
fabrics, walls, and
tabletops. Here are
seven ways to bring dark
corners into the light.

1 entry table

Make small changes
when the spring
decorating bug bites.
Round up fresh items
to put a new face on an
entry. Signs of spring are
easy to create: pastel
blooms in a wicker
basket, pale landscapes
hung on the wall, and
small reminders of
vacations arranged on
a bamboo table that's
tucked just inside
the door.

2 outdoor tea

Set a tea table on a porch or veranda. Here's a quick way to clean silver for your outdoor tea: Line a sink or plastic tub with aluminum foil and pour in a cup of Tide (no other detergent seems to work). Fill the tub with warm water. Slip the silver pieces under water and leave overnight. In the morning, they'll emerge clean and bright, the tarnish now magnetically clinging to the foil.

3 matching prints

Cover a wall with the same fabric as a chair. First, attach firring strips to the wall along the ceiling and wainscot. Then add vertical strips at intervals that measure slightly less than the width of the fabric (use a level to ensure straightness). Beginning at the center of the wall, staple the top edge of a fabric panel at the ceiling. Fasten at the wainscot. Working toward the corners, repeat the process to cover the wall (overlap vertical edges along the firring strips). Cover the staple lines and raw edges of the fabric with glued-on gimp.

4 tray collection

To corral a small-scale collection that's on the loose, use a tray to organize and display it. For example, a passion for ticking clocks can result in several scattered about the house. Massed on a tray, they create a bigger decorative impact than they do as singles. Also, the setting of the collection is important. Here, where clocks are useful as timekeepers, the display makes a witty statement.

print 5 power

Layer texture, color, and pattern to bring spring to a dormant corner. Begin with two or three colors. For example, purple, pink, and beige are the color keys to the successful gathering of items shown here. To get started, choose a printed fabric that carries several colors and inspires you to redecorate. Keep the colors in mind as you pull together pretty and practical pieces for a bedside stand, a side table in the living room, or a pleasing display on a kitchen ledge.

vintage 6 white

Paint a dark wooden dresser white to perk up its graceful shape and curvy lines. White paint always works to breathe new life into a tired, dark piece of furniture. To find candidates for freshening with white paint, search flea markets, farm sales, estate sales, antiques shops, and secondhand thrift stores. This dresser came from an auction of old hotel furnishings. Clean the surface of the piece with soap and water to remove grease and dust. Then clean it with a lint-free cloth. Prime the surface with a high-quality latex primer and finish it with two coats of a good-quality white latex enamel. Clean up with water.

floral room fresheners

To make a guest bedroom new for spring, gather a basket of floral fabrics to spread around the room. Lay a needlepoint rug beside the bed and find pretty, hand-embroidered pillowcases in a secondhand shop. Add big impact with a floral coverlet at the end of the bed and lean floral pillows against the embroidered white linens. When guests arrive, treat them to a bedside arrangement: a brilliant bouquet and a floral teacup for a refined and totally feminine touch.

stretch
a space

Come out of winter's tight, warm nest and spread your decorating wings. It's time to live bigger. Open windows for fresh air and remove heavy window coverings that hide the reviving landscape. If the view isn't all that great or you need window coverings for privacy, spring for a white scrim of new ready-made sheers. You'll find them at low, low prices in the home furnishings sections of discount stores.

Pull comfortable chairs around a coffee table. Fluff up the overall scene with pillows covered in light-spirited plaids, prints, and stripes. Eliminate winter's clutter by returning books to bookcases and emptying containers on tables so they are ready for new items that come with wider living. Take advantage of nature's new growth and grace your rooms with expansive, casual bouquets placed in large cylinders. Sit back, stretch out, and survey the beauty of your home, sweet home.

Spring forward with an earlier-rising sun and a clock set to daylight saving time. Spend the extra hours investing in your existing real estate, expanding its potential for bigger, better, and more relaxed living.

Add a room inside a room. An L-shape room is the perfect candidate for tucking in an extra stretch-out space. Cordon off the short end of the "L" with a curtain cable (available in a kit from home centers or hardware stores), 24 clip rings, and 16 yards of frothy scrim fabric from the drapery section of a fabric store. Strung wall-to-wall in shower-curtain style, the filmy privacy curtain cocoons sweet dreams and rustles romantically whenever the spring wind stirs its gentle folds.

Slide a sleigh bed into the nook to provide for soft landings. It serves as a sofa by day and a napping spot anytime the mood is right. Add a trundle under the bed to extend the sleeping space for guests. Use the main part of the room for other purposes, such as an office, sewing room, studio, or living space. If the L-shape room is large enough, it can become an entire suite for guests.

Make more space available on top of a coffee table by reorganizing. Gather small objects on a large tray instead of strewing them haphazardly across the table's surface.

Arrange dozens of blooms in a silver compote for a compact and effusive spring display. If you use enough flowers, they'll hold each other in place without florist's foam.

Bring outdoor elements inside to psychologically expand your space. Garden signs, such as the iron arch shown, keep wide-open spaces and images in mind.

Decorate a side porch to gain dining space. Choose a round table; it seats more people and allows a more fluid traffic flow than square or rectangular tables.

Bring a pillowed settee to the table for comfortable and expansive seating. Fill the room with fresh green fabrics and cover the windows with curtains for privacy.

Replace an existing table that crowds a small kitchen with a flip-top bar or half-round table. Fold up the chairs and the wall-hung table when they're not in use.

Create stretch-out space with a hammock and easygoing rocking chairs on a porch or breezeway. Or make use of outdoor spaces between the house and garage.

Fill the hammock with pillows and a lightweight quilt. Place a bench between the hammock and chairs to work as a coffee table. Hang lanterns overhead for magic.

Tie fabric pinafores on rocking chairs to add a little print pizzazz to an easy-living space. Patterns for slipcovers are found in home decorating pattern books.

grow a
garden

knot garden

Create a miniature version of an English herb garden with this dish planter made from the top of a plastic birdbath.

materials:

- 24-inch-diameter plastic birdbath
- drill; handsaw
- scissors; silk pins; plastic wrap
- 24-inch square of stiff white paper
- potting soil; annual rye grass seed
- reindeer moss; small pebbles
- small topiary in urn

Drill five drainage holes in the birdbath saucer with a ½-inch-diameter woodworker's drill. Cut out the top part of the center support in the saucer with a saw.

Fill the birdbath saucer with soil. Lay the paper stencil pattern over the soil (see tools and tips 101 for instructions on making the pattern), centering it and securing it with silk pins. Sprinkle grass seed generously over the stencil. Brush the excess seed onto the soil. Carefully remove the stencil. Cover loosely with plastic wrap. Water the soil from the bottom until the seeds sprout. Keep the garden in a sunny location.

Trim the grass with scissors when it has grown a few inches. Fill in the triangular sections of the knot design with reindeer moss. Place the topiary in the center of the saucer garden and press small pebbles into the soil around the edge.

skill level: beginner

tools and tips 101

To make the garden stencil for sowing the grass seed, enlarge the pattern, *left*. To do so, fold the 24-inch square of stiff paper in half. Have an imaging center or quick-copy store enlarge the half-pattern to fit the size of the folded paper. Transfer the enlarged half-pattern to the folded paper and cut out the stencil (the shaded area in the pattern) with scissors.

If you wish to use a birdbath of a different size, adjust the pattern size accordingly by using a square of paper whose sides equal the diameter of the birdbath.

mosaic planter

Want that summer-garden feeling before it arrives? Sink your hands

in warm soil after you complete this easy project.

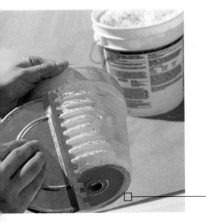

materials:

- terra-cotta pot
- white acrylic or latex paint; paintbrush
- notched trowel
- tile adhesive
- seashells
- gray grout
- sponge; clean cloth

Paint the pot white and let it dry. Using the trowel, spread tile adhesive over a section of the pot.

Press shells into the adhesive either in rows (shown in the finished pot here) or in a random design. Fit the shells as closely together as possible. For large, hollow shells, fill the shell with adhesive to help it hold better. Repeat the adhesive and shell-placing process until the pot is covered. Let the adhesive dry completely, checking to see that all the shells are securely attached and making spot repairs wherever you find a loose piece.

Spread and press grout between the shells with a damp sponge. Clean the sponge with water as necessary. After the grout dries, polish away the haze left on the seashells with a soft cloth.

skill level: beginner

tools and tips 101

Gather your own seashells or buy them at a crafts store. Or order them from online sources (see Buying Guide, page 184). Choose from a large assortment of small and medium-size shells. The best buy is the bulk bag of assorted shells; you'll get shells that look much like the ones used for this project.

You'll find tile adhesive and grout in kitchen and bathroom remodeling supply stores or in the tile sections of home improvement stores. Notched trowels can be found in the same places. Locate terra-cotta pots in garden stores and nurseries.

- **20-inch×95-inch silk scarf** (available in fashion accessory departments and stores)
- **2 pierced earring hooks** (available in jewelry-making sections of crafts stores)
- **sewing thread**
- **2 wall-hanging hooks**

Sew earring hooks on one long edge of the scarf, placing a hook 25 inches from each end of the scarf.

Fasten the wall hooks into the window trim. To allow for a slight drape when the scarf is hung, place the wall hooks 2 inches closer together than the distance between the earring hooks on the scarf. Slip the earring hooks on the wall hooks.

skill level: beginner

brighten
a window

scarf shade

ribbon tabbed

materials:

- 15 yards of 2-inch-wide voile ribbon
- curtain rod and brackets
- two 48-inch-wide cotton voile panels 10 inches longer than the window frame
- sewing thread; silk pins

Hang the curtain rod following the package instructions. Cut the ribbon into ten 1½-yard lengths.

Hem the sides and bottoms of each panel with narrow hems. Fold the tops over ¼ inch; press. Fold again 3 inches, press, and sew along the inner folded edges. Press three 3-inch-wide pleats into the panel tops. Pin and sew a ribbon length to the back of each pleat. Leaving a 9-inch-long loop at the top for the tab, stitch each ribbon length to the front of each pleat. Add a ribbon tab to each corner of each curtain panel.

Slide the ribbon loops over the rod; tie loose knots 6 inches from the ends of each ribbon on the fronts of the panels.

skill level: intermediate

layered look

materials:

- 2 panels of printed cotton voile 12 inches longer than the window frame; sewing thread
- 2 tension rods
- white sheer ready-made curtain

To sew rod pockets on the top of each voile panel, fold over raw edges ¼ inch and press; fold over again 2½ inches and press. Sew close to the twice-folded edge. For the top of the rod pocket, sew 1 inch from the top edge of each panel.

Sew rod sleeves. Cut a 4-inch-wide strip from the bottom of each voile panel. Fold over the long raw edges ¼ inch; press. Fold each strip in half lengthwise; press. Sew close to the two edges. Hem the panels with narrow hems.

Hang the white sheer curtain against the window. Slip the sleeves onto the second rod and add a voile panel on each side. Hang the rod in front of the white sheer.

skill level: beginner

materials:

- eight 24-inch-square pieces of cotton voile in a variety of colors
- sewing thread
- wall hooks
- tension rods
- plastic shower curtain clips in a coordinating color

Hem cotton voile squares with narrow rolled hems. To make a rolled hem, fold over all raw edges ¼ inch and press. Fold over again and press. Sew close to the edge of the folds.

Hang the wall hooks on the window frame, spacing them 3 inches apart.

Hang the curtains. Set tension rods into the window frame. Lay the hanky-style squares over the rods, pulling them at angles for a casual, layered look. Hang the corners of the remaining squares from the hooks with shower curtain clips.

skill level: beginner

brighten a window

hanky panky

london blind

materials:

- 1½ yards of yellow voile (fits 36-inch-wide × 40-inch-long window)
- 1½ yards of white voile (lining)
- 1 yard of hook-and-loop fastening tape; sewing thread; staple gun
- 1"×2"×3' pine board (mounting)
- eight 1-inch-diameter cafe rings
- 1-inch nails; 2 screw eyes
- 6 yards 2½-inch-wide voile ribbon

Cut the voile into two pieces 1 inch wider than the outside measurement of the window and 18 inches longer. Right sides facing, sew sides and bottom with ½-inch seams. Turn and press. Sew one side of hook-and-loop tape across top of panel back. Hand-stitch cafe rings in two vertical rows on the panel back, 9 inches from the sides and 12 inches apart.

Fasten screw eyes to the mounting board aligned with the ring rows. Staple remaining fastening strip on the board top; mount the board on the window with nails. Cut ribbon length in half. Tie ribbon ends to bottom rings; thread upward through rings and screw eyes. Thread right ribbon through left screw eye; pull down to gather shade.

skill level: intermediate

materials:

- 2½ yards of 45-inch-wide cotton voile
- sewing thread; needle
- 3 packages of beads
- tension rod

Hem the top and bottom edges of the fabric panel with narrow, rolled hems.

Trim both ends of the panel with a beaded border, spacing the bead strands 2 inches apart. To make a bead strand, thread a needle and slide one bead onto the strand; knot. Thread enough beads onto the strand to make it 2½ inches long. Fasten the strand to the hem of the fabric panel. Repeat until both hems are bordered.

Hang the curtain by slipping it over the tension rod, gathering it slightly, and pulling it at an angle.

skill level: beginner

beaded panel

make a
statement piece

windowed cupboard

Make something new from something old—turn a window into a door on a cupboard you build yourself. Adjust these instructions to the window you choose.

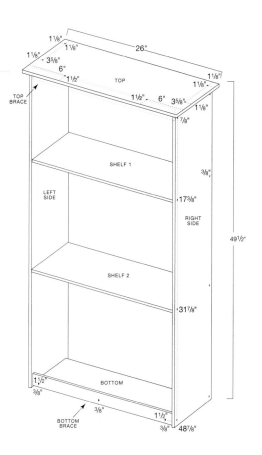

materials:

- 24-inch ×46-inch salvage window
- $\frac{1}{2}$-inch × 6-inch × 4-foot poplar board (shelves)
- 1-inch × 8-inch × 3-foot poplar board (top)
- 1-inch × 6-inch × 2-foot poplar board (bottom)
- two 1-inch × 6-inch × 5-foot poplar boards (sides)
- two 1-inch × 4-inch × 2-foot poplar boards (top/bottom braces)
- 1-inch × 2-inch × 2-foot poplar board (back brace)
- 48-inch × 24¾-inch beaded-board panel (back)
- twenty-nine #8 1½-inch wood screws; nails; sandpaper; wood filler
- white semigloss latex paint; paintbrush
- drawer pull; two flush hinges; one catch

Cut the boards as follows: *For the two shelves,* cut the 4-foot-long board in half. *For the cupboard top,* cut the 3-foot board to 26 inches and rip the width to 6½ inches. *For the cupboard bottom,* cut the 2-foot-long board to 23¼ inches long and rip the 6-inch-wide width to 4¾ inches. *For the sides,* cut the 5-foot-long boards to 49¼ inches. *For the top and bottom braces,* cut the two 2-foot-long boards to 23¼ inches long and rip the 4-inch-wide widths to 1¾ inches. *For the back brace,* cut the 2-inch-wide board to 23¼ inches long. Sand all pieces.

Drill holes for screws, using a #8x1¼-inch countersinking tool. *On the cupboard top,* drill two holes 1⅛ inches from each end and 1⅛ inches from the board's back edge. Also drill two holes 1⅛ inch from the end and 3⅝ inches from the back edge. Along the front edge, drill two holes 6 inches from the board end and 1½ inches from the front edge. *On each side piece,* drill eight holes (four on each side) ⅜ inch from the front and back edges at the following distances from the top of the board: ⅞ inch, 17⅜ inches, 31⅞ inches, and 48⅞ inches. On the top and bottom braces, drill three holes ⅜ inch from one edge at 1½ inches from each end and at center. Assemble the cupboard according to the diagram, *above right,* using wood screws. Fill the screw holes with wood filler; let dry, and sand. Nail the beaded-board panel to the back. Paint the cupboard and window white.

Attach the window by screwing the flat hinges to the window where the shelves meet the side of the cupboard; fasten the hinges to the cupboard. Center the catch at the front edge of the cupboard's inside wall and attach the drawer pull to the window frame.

skill level: advanced

faux fireplace

Assemble two columns, a header, and a shelf to create a focal-point

fireplace surround from home store or lumberyard boards.

materials:

- two 1-inch × 8-inch × 6-foot pine select boards (shelf, header)
- 1-inch × 8-inch × 6-foot #2 pine board (underpinnings)
- four 6¼-inch × 8-inch decorative blocks
- 7 feet of pilaster molding (columns)
- 8 feet of 5-inch-wide large dentil crown molding (shelf)
- forty #8 1¼-inch wood screws
- twenty 1-inch trim nails
- sandpaper; semigloss latex paint; paintbrush

For the mantel shelf, cut one pine select board to 60 inches long. For the bottom cover, from #2 pine, cut a piece 2¾ inches wide by 51¹⁄₁₆ inches long. Also cut five 2⅞-inches × 2¾-inches support blocks from #2 pine. Fasten the support blocks at the back of the mantel shelf underside; fasten the bottom cover temporarily over the supports. For decorative molding, cut a 58-inch-long front and two 6¼-inch-long ends from dentil molding. Miter the cut ends at a 45-degree angle (overall length should be 58 inches from the longest tips of the mitered angles). Miter the side pieces to match the front (overall length should be 6¼ inches at longest points of angles). Sand all pieces. Match up the mitered corners of the molding, keeping flats of molding tight against edge of bottom cover and underside of mantel shelf. Molding should be centered if bottom cover board and support blocks are correctly positioned. Begin tacking side piece of molding into place, mated with center molding. Repeat for other side. Sink nails into place using nail set when fit is obtained.

For the header, cut one pine select board to 50 inches long (face board). Router a seat ¼ inch deep and 6 inches wide into both ends. Drill four countersink holes into the back side of the face board equidistant from edges on routered region. Sand. Position decorative block tightly against routered step (block should extend ¼ inch past end of face board and ¾ inch below bottom edge). Fasten with screws.

For the columns, cut pilaster molding into two 41¹⁵⁄₁₆-inch pieces. Router a seat ¼ inch deep and ¾ inch long at one end of each column, removing the ribs from the face of the board. On the other ends of the boards, router a seat ¼ inch deep and 8 inches wide. Drill four countersink holes into the backs of the columns, position decorative blocks tightly against the ribs in the 8-inch-deep seat, and fasten with wood screws. Sand. Paint surround sections in desired color.

To assemble, place header facedown on flat surface. Place a column section at each end of the header to create a U-shape. Position columns so that routered seat matches up with ¾-inch block overage. Drill two countersink holes into back side of each column. Fasten with wood screws. Fasten securely to wall with screws. To mount the shelf over the header, fasten a horizontal line of four 9-inch-long pieces of #2 pine on the wall in positions to receive the shelf between the support blocks (use a level). Fasten the shelf to the tops of the wall attachment boards at the back.

skill level: advanced

poster bed finish

Give a plain pine bed the look of jasperware pottery with a textured blue paint finish and glued-on, carved hardwood cutouts.

materials:

- unfinished pine bed
- sandpaper
- primer; paintbrush
- gallon of light blue latex paint
- pint of silica sand
- white acrylic paint; small paintbrush
- wood cutouts; wood glue

Sand and prime the bed to prepare it for two coats of paint. (The first coat is a blend of latex paint and silica sand that creates a rough finish reminiscent of jasperware pottery; the second coat is plain paint to make the color consistent.)

Mix the silica sand with a half gallon of the blue paint. Stir well. Paint the bed with the mixture, stirring it continuously to keep the sandy texture even while applying the mix. Dry overnight. Apply a second coat of the remaining half gallon of plain blue paint to the bed.

Paint the wood cutouts with white acrylic paint. When dry, attach them to the bed with wood glue. Use them sparingly on the broad, flat surfaces of the bed to avoid making the decorative look of the bed too busy.

skill level: beginner

tools and tips 101

Silica sand or gel is a colloidal silica that resembles coarse white sand in appearance. It possesses many fine pores that make it extremely absorbent. You'll find it in crafts stores in the floral section because it's often used by floral designers to dry flowers. When fresh blossoms are buried in silica sand for a period of days, the sand absorbs the moisture from the flowers while preserving their colors.

The look of wood carvings is easier to obtain now than it was long ago, when decorative pieces were hand-carved with a knife. Today, the look of wood carving is inexpensive and available through molded wood pulp and machined pieces. These are sold separately in decorative sections of home building and remodeling centers.

autumn

Rearranging furniture is an effective and inexpensive way to freshen a room as the seasons turn. Here's a possible scenario: Let's say your living room is composed of a sofa, two chairs and tables, windows, and a fireplace. For fall, you keep the sofa in its summertime position, but remove its light-colored slipcover (see summer, *page 49*). You move the floor screen to the side to reveal part of the fireplace and add small decorative touches, such as leafy lampshades, pumpkins, dried hydrangeas, and soft pillows, to fill the room with warmth.

In winter, you move the seating group so it faces the fireplace (revealed by moving the screen into a large doorway). The screen works to shield the seating group and draw it close to the fire while the traffic flows around the back of the seating pieces. You change autumn's leafy lampshades for winter-white ones and hang a salvaged pediment "mantel" on your featureless fireplace. A string of votive candles on the temporary mantel and a pillar group on the coffee table add the warmth and power of fire to the cold comforts of winter.

When spring comes, pull the furniture away from the closed-down fireplace and turn your attention to outdoor living spaces. But don't ignore the living room. Winter's rug is replaced with a sunnier one, and a pale yellow sofa wrap comes out to lighten the room. Candles are removed, garden flowers come in, and tabletops are reorganized and simplified. Winter's clutter is put away in response to unexpected urges to clean.

spring

By summer, the living room is easy. You move the seating group away from the fireplace, facing it toward windows and greener views. The folding screen now completely hides the fireplace, and the main feature of the room is its sunlight, bare wooden floor—and simplified decorating. If you maintain this simplicity all summer, you'll feel the contrast when autumn returns with its abundant decorating scheme.

summer

Stretch out on white sands to watch clouds drift by. At night, stare up at the stars for signs of the future. Then, if it's not too much trouble, simplify your home for the sultry season by stripping it down to the bare necessities. Kick back on a sofa, a chaise, or a hammock because summer's lazy days require less than strenuous decorating efforts.

summer

On the next pages, you'll find the easiest of decorating ideas.

color it lively

Call it a child's watercolor or a wildflower garden. No matter how it's assembled, summer's color palette adds up to a happy blend of innocence and freedom. Its painterly backdrop colors are naturally cool and relaxing, like blue skies and white clouds, aqualine beaches and white surf. Then sandy beiges, pale corals, and cool greens invite you to settle in. Finally, the whole composition is punched up with bright accents blazing with energy—like hot red zinnias, seductive pink roses, vibrant yellow sunflowers, and myriad fanciful flowers. If you're the summerhouse type, these are the colors to live by.

White walls and woodwork lace this room as clouds lace the sky, and pale wood-toned floors have the open comfort of a sandy beach. The only accent color in this summer room is a medium-bright blue because the decorative intent is to create freshness and light and a soft place to land. For a more exciting room, increase the intensity of its colors by adding small, bright pieces on ledges and tabletops, in bookcases, and on chairs.

White, the great noncolor of the summer palette, works as the perfect backdrop. It brings with it a fresh air of quiet relaxation and plenty of space to breathe. Literally the absence of color, white reflects and frames real colors, showing them off to their best advantage and providing a blank canvas on which to play. When you begin a new color scheme, paint your walls white. Then experiment with fabrics and accessories to gain courage in handling color.

Wicker furniture, *opposite,* is practical in humid climates because it needs moisture to keep from becoming brittle. It's also easy to repaint when refurbishing is needed or when a change of color is desired.

Custom-made to double as a king-size sleeper, this wicker sofa, *right,* is covered in a hardy fabric to protect against sand, saltwater, and spills. Instead of brilliant colors for focal-point punch, small-scale patterns on pillow fabrics accomplish the same effect. Washable coral-tone rugs soften and lighten the bare floor.

The most stunning accessories in and around this house have been provided by Mother Nature herself. Scarlet geraniums, blazing bougainvillea, and hot pink impatiens, *left*, thrive in the moist air almost year-round. The vibrant blossoms offer contrast to the soft, cool blues and whites of the surf.

Just inside kitchen windows that look out on a sunny courtyard, *opposite*, bright green and yellow ceramic-tiled countertops underscore the tomato reds, corn yellows, and artichoke greens of meal preparations. The constantly changing parade of fruits, vegetables, painted pottery, and printed towels moving through the small kitchen keeps it alive with natural, free-wheeling color.

A summer color scheme is an opportunity for fun. Once you think of your home as an artist's white canvas and paint your walls and woodwork accordingly, overlay the large blocks of white with smaller portions of medium-toned hues. Color countertops, tables, chair coverings, rugs, and bed coverings with mid-range colors, saving intense shades for small bits of brightness on accent pillows, art pieces, dishes, flower bouquets, and bowls of fruit. Just follow nature's color formula: 50 parts pale (as in sky and sea) to 10 parts medium bright or dark (as in stone and vegetation) to one part saturated intensity (as in fruit and flower).

Because a few sizzling summer colors go a long way, keep your color scheme balanced by using generous amounts of light, cooling hues. Whether you're inspired by the expanses of sky and sea, the awesome neutrals of mountain and desert, or endless amber waves of grain, relaxing soft colors will ease you into decorating success.

Salty breezes waft through this master bedroom, *opposite,* where a large white sleigh bed is piled high for cool seaside nights. Even without the sea at your door, you can enjoy a seaside decorating style by adding breezy cabana stripes, ocean-wave quilts, and shuttered windows that flirt with the rise and fall of the sun.

Adirondack chairs, *above,* are classics that furnish getaways in the out-of-doors. Seal them into their natural wood tones or paint them green for woodland settings. For a waterside adventure (or the feeling of one), paint them white or bright.

open up

Be practical—sunbathe while you plan your next decorating move. Here are seven sun-inspired decorating ideas to contemplate on a beachside chaise. Once you visualize the steps you'll take to hang breezy curtains, create bookends, and set summer tables, it'll take no time at all to get up and do.

1 breezeway

Hang a wind drape to celebrate summer's breezes. To make it, loop fabric-store ribbons of varying widths over a tension rod in a doorway. Hold the ribbons in place by hot-gluing them to a horizontal ribbon. For a fanciful border, glue on fun trims, such as this chorus line of starfish.

sand bucket bookend

To keep books in line on open shelves, create personal ways to support the stack. For a summer reading shelf, fill a bucket with sand for weight and add a starfish. Other bookend ideas: Finish a cookbook collection with a heavy box or small bin filled with books. Or use a ceramic cookie jar or a saltine canister filled with pickling salt. For science books, position large agate or quartz stones as bookends. Hold vintage books in place with salvaged architectural brackets.

sun3spot

Turn winter's warm cocoon of a bed into an open-air spa. First, stash heavy bedding in summer storage drawers and cover the bed with lightweight, 100-percent cotton sheets and cover-ups. (Cotton is known for its easy-breathing, cool qualities.) Remove heavy curtains or decorative side panels for the simpler look of roll-up blinds already in use under the winter window dressings. They're perfect for privacy when you need it or for a sun shield when the temperatures are just too high. Pull winter rugs from the floor so you can feel the cool, smooth comfort of hardwood floors under your bare feet. The change will do you good.

4 spaced-out blooms

Showcase individual blooms by transforming an antique milk carrier (or an old utensil tray, soda crate, or wine rack) into a corral for summer's lighthearted blooms. Outfit the containers with empty wine carafes, milk bottles, or jelly jars. Then add water, tall grasses, and whatever hardy stems catch your eye.

5 open shelving

Push back the walls in a tiny bathroom to make extra storage in the tub area. The time for this project is when you're replacing the bathroom walls. Cut 1-inch pine boards to fit between two wall studs at the end of the tub. Set the board shelves in place on tiny wood blocks nailed into the studs. Frame around the area after new walls are installed. Fill nail holes with spackling compound and paint with two coats to finish.

6 sun shower

Hang a transparent curtain over the window in a tub and shower area. While finding successful window treatments for this decorating problem is difficult, this idea works perfectly to protect the wall and window frame from shower spray. The bonus (provided privacy isn't an issue) is that you can stand in the shimmer of sunlight while you shower.

white7hot style

Set an outdoor table with a white cloth, a centerpiece of glass, and plastic tableware (plastic has never looked so good). If you place the table under a structure, you can create an open-air pavilion by hanging ready-made cotton tab curtains from lumber store closet poling. Purchase closet hardware kits to hang the poles in the pavilion structure. Add inexpensive white deck chairs. For magic, burn gel candles set in bowls of water and hang an antique chandelier from the ceiling of the outdoor structure on a chain and an S hook.

add white

Lighten a room for summer with white, a simple way to get a sophisticated yet carefree look. For example, remove heavy winter draperies to reveal more of a room's white-painted walls and woodwork. The room will also feel more spacious. If you feel uncomfortable with bare windows, change heavy coverings to light lifts of ready-made lace paneling threaded on tension rods. Adjust the lengths of the tension rods to fit the windows and fasten them between the sides of the window frames.

Slipcover dark, wintry upholstery, pillows, and cushions with white. Cotton canvas duck or cotton brocade slipcovers lighten a room and give it a fresh, easygoing attitude. Despite the pristine look, white slipcovers are perfect for summer use because the fabrics are washable and feel comfortable to the skin. To purchase or make slipcovers, check catalogs and pattern counters in fabric stores.

Sunshine is at home in a room filled with white paint, furniture, accessories, and fabrics. In such a place, it plays across a room, catches objects on a table, and prints their images on the wall. Take note of these magical movements as part of summer's decorating fun.

Lighten a dining room with white paint, glass, and shine. Create a tone-on-tone color scheme for subtle contrast on walls. Here, high wainscoting and moldings are stark white while the upper walls hint at a cool, earthy green. Open shelving hangs on walls for practical and decorative reasons: Glassware is easily accessible to the table and, at the same time, it adds a beautiful display of transparent objects and bright shimmer to the room. Likewise, choose glass bottles and other unusual glass containers for vases when you bring in flowers from the garden. The glitter and transparency of water in glass infuse the room with freshness.

Polish doors and woodwork with white enamel. Enamel is washable and white gloss, like shining glass, contributes to the light, clean attitude of summer. For special effects, remove boring, characterless core doors from a room and replace them with more interesting doors from salvage yards and shops. Carry a tape measure while you shop so you'll be sure to get the height, width, and thickness measurements correct. While you're at it, pick up salvage doorknobs that are thrilling to the touch and add more character to your new (old) doors.

Trade in clumsy dining chairs for comfortable, lightweight wicker chairs. Heavy, hard-to-move pieces never have a place at a table, so keep easy wicker working year-round. The summery greens and yellows of these chairs echo the upper walls of the room and work well for the winter season too.

Use a tablecloth in fresh colors to hide the leggy look of many chairs around a table. Washable cotton duck or white canvas is a good underlay cloth, while a washable green and white vintage cloth whisks off for washing.

Sheers have come a long, stylish way from the time when they were tucked discreetly behind pinch-pleat draperies. Now they stand on their own. Use them to build a white backdrop for a sunny getaway or reading corner. Sew 2-inch-wide rod pockets into two 45-inch-wide panels of soft, white-patterned sheer fabric and hang them on a tension rod in a window frame. Or hang ready-made cafe curtains in the window.

Hang sheers from floor to ceiling on slim curtain cable wire to carve an intimate alcove out of a nondescript room. The result is instant architecture. All-cotton sheers with a Swiss plaid have the right weight and translucency to serve as wall partitions that don't block the light. Their hint of color and pattern provides just enough structure to keep the room from being too undefined.

Accent the room with white fabrics decorated in small amounts of a color that coordinates with the sheer partitions.

Close the partitions for privacy; open them for company. When others come to your sheer sanctuary, they can pull up chairs around a table. You can also use the space as a casual office.

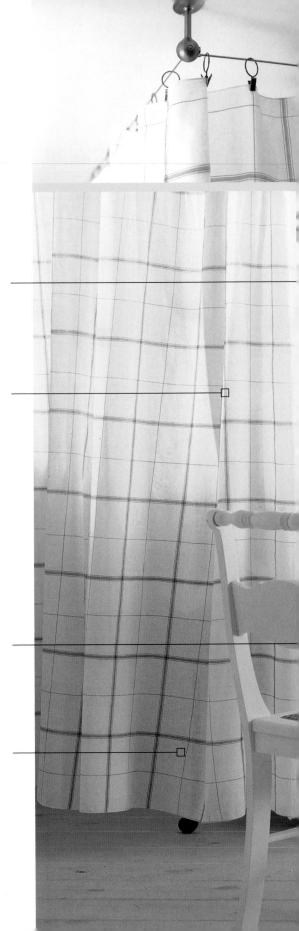

New hardware choices make decorating with sheers simpler than ever. Metal brackets strung with wire cable are a less clunky alternative to rods; clip rings are no-fuss fasteners. Both are available from most window treatment catalogs and decorating superstores.

upsy daisy

sparkle
and shine

materials:

- plate rail
- antique dresser mirror with legs
- drill
- long screws
- screwdriver
- wood filler or spackling compound
- paint
- paintbrush
- sandpaper

Recycle an abandoned dresser mirror by hanging it upside down from a plate rail attached to the wall. Hanging techniques will vary with the mirror's structure and how it was originally attached to the furniture. Here, the "feet" of the mirror were fitted to a plate rail by notching them at the back so they fit snugly around the bottom of the plate rail. Drill and screw the legs to the plate rail's base molding to secure the mirror.

Fill the screw holes with wood filler or spackling compound. Sand smooth; paint the mirror frame the same color as the rest of the woodwork for a unified look.

skill level: intermediate

multi-mirrors

materials:

- **8 picture frames with precut mats**
- **mirror panels for 8 frames**
- **straightedge (optional)**
- **glass cutter (optional)**
- **level**
- **ruler**

Remove the glass from the picture frames and use the panes as measurements for the mirrors. Have a mirror cut for each frame at a frame store, home improvement center, or custom-mirror store. Or cut the pieces from mirror tile yourself, using a straightedge and a glass cutter. (Wear eye protection and heavy gloves when cutting mirror.)

Reassemble the frames, inserting the mirror panels in place of the glass panels that came with the frames. Replace the picture frame backs.

Hang the frames on the wall, leaving 1½-inch gaps between each pair. Use a level and ruler to ensure straightness and correct measurements.

skill level: beginner

sparkle and shine

mirrored door

Turn a plain interior door into an intriguing "passageway" by creating a fool-the-eye French door from a mirror and muntins.

materials:
- custom-cut mirror panel
- pop-in muntins
- miter or circular saw
- roll of double-stick cushioned tape
- 6 mirror clips
- screwdriver; clippers

Measure the door to determine the size of mirror you will order. First measure the height and width of the door. Then subtract measurements that will leave a border on all sides of the mirror equal to about one-sixth the door's length or width. Have a mirror cut to size (see tools and tips 101). If necessary, trim the muntins with a miter or circular saw so the ends are equal to the outside measurements of the mirror. Adhere the muntins to the mirror with double-stick cushioned tape cut into small pieces and evenly spaced along the back of the muntins.

Mount the mirror to the door with six mirror clips, placing them about 3 inches in from each corner and midway on each vertical side. Set the mirror in place under the clips (two sets of hands are best at this point) and use a screwdriver to gently tighten the clips.

skill level: beginner

tools and tips 101

You'll find everything you need for this project at large home improvement centers or hardware stores. Muntins are available in the window and door section; mirror clips and custom mirror cutting are available in the glass-cutting area. Talk to a store employee about cutting the mirror panel. A slightly more expensive option is to have a glass and mirror store cut the mirror for you.

An alternative to glass mirror is a plastic reflective material known as acrylic mirror, available at home improvement centers. To cut the panel yourself, use a straightedge and a sharp utility knife to score along an edge. Then bend the material until it snaps apart along the scored line.

1 lanterns

Hang a collection of paper shades fitted with battery-operated lights for a sparkling backyard evening or picnic at the beach. Beyond the fire safety bonus they give you, battery-operated lanterns may be placed anywhere you please. To hang them, use long strands of white ribbon that will float over a pretty table and flit about in the breeze.

chase

fireflies

birdbath lights

Settle a large decorative bowl of water into a birdbath stand or fill the birdbath bowl with water. Add a few smooth rocks for interest and float flower-shaped votive candles on the water (white candles are particularly effective in the evening). Sprinkle a few tiny garden blooms between the candles. When the wicks burn down to a fizzle in the water, replenish the fire bath with more votive candles.

3

fire and ice

Combine candles and sea glass in a planter to set a magical scene for an outdoor gathering. First, lean a large mirror on a buffet table set against a wall. The mirror will act as a backdrop, doubling the number of firelights and reflecting the view of the outdoor space. Fill a planter with sea glass, insert tall tapers, and light the wicks. The buffet will attract your guests like moths to the flame.

4

hurricane pots

Set several small, medium, and large terra-cotta pots at an entry or along stairs to light the way to a garden party. Fill the pots with sand from a nursery or home center and set large white pillar candles in the sand. Lower hurricane glasses over the candles and light the wicks. Add small votive candles along ledges to supplement the firefly effect.

blooming 5 chandelier

Turn a hanging planter into a garden light by adding tiny bulbs at the top of the hanger. To make the lighting mechanism shown here, gather a string of miniature Christmas tree or outdoor garden lights (these came with white reflective shades) into a tight bundle with the extra loops of wire gathered together at the top and the light bulbs spread loosely at the bottom. Wire the light-string bundle securely at the looped-wire end. Then fan the lights around the planter at the point where the hanger meets the hanging chain. Add a wide ribbon or tulle bow to hide the wiring.

make a
splash

color-crazy canopy

Take a plunge—splash color on an outdoor dining area. You'll need a table that's set inside a gazebo, under a tree, or under an arbor.

materials:

- 4 yards of 36-inch-wide tablecloth plastic
- paper punch; scissors
- three 36-inch-long bamboo poles
- 6 yards of ¼-inch-wide white ribbon
- six 1- or 2-inch-diameter eye screws (to fit the diameter of the bamboo pole ends)

To make the pole-carrying holes in the canopy, fold the plastic strip in half crosswise (canopy center). Placing the paper punch over the fold as far as it will go, punch a set of holes through the plastic 1 inch from each side of the strip and every 8½ inches along the fold (five sets of holes). Fold the canopy crosswise 20 inches from each end and repeat to make three bands of holes.

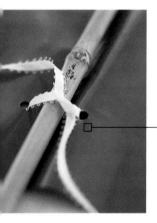

Lay each bamboo pole between a band of holes. Slip a 12-inch length of white ribbon through each set of punched holes and knot the ribbon ends securely.

Set three pairs of eye screws 34 inches apart on each overhead beam. Hang the center rod of the canopy first, slipping the ends of the poles through the eyes of the screws. See other hanging options under tools and tips 101.

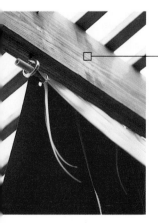

skill level: beginner

You may need to adapt the canopy hanging to fit a dining structure if it isn't like the one shown here. For a sturdy, windproof option, hang the rods through screw eyes set in the structure and tie them securely with ribbons. Or if wind isn't a problem and you want an intimate canopy hanging low over the table, lower the canopy poles on decorative ribbon loops tied through the screw eyes. For hanging the canopy from a loose structure, such as a tree, adapt the ribbon-loop tying technique, raising and lowering the lengths until the desired height is achieved. If you're in a public park that can't be marred but has a beamed dining structure, loop the ribbons around the beams to hang the bamboo poles.

striped wall

Decorate a white wall with wide and narrow bands of color. Paint the wide bands a cool purple, the narrow ones a tart, apple green.

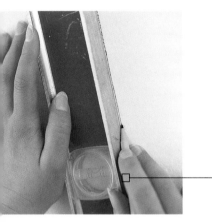

materials:

- 2 flat latex interior paints in coordinating colors
- woodworker's level; ruler
- sharp, hard-lead pencil
- 2-inch-wide low-tack painter's tape
- paint tray
- 7-inch-wide paint roller

Measure and mark the first stripe at the center of the white-painted wall. To find the placement for the first mark, divide the length of the wall in half to find the center of the first (18-inch-wide) stripe. Then mark the wall 9 inches to the left or right of the center of the stripe. With a level indicating vertical straightness, mark the wall lightly with a pencil along the level's edge.

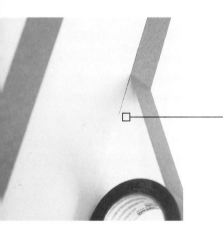

Place painter's tape along the pencil line on the outside edge of the stripe. See tools and tips 101 for two tape-applying methods. When the first tape is fastened, measure for the next (9-inch-wide) stripe, beginning at the unmarked side of the painter's tape. Repeat the marking and taping to complete the wall. If desired, continue around the corners.

Paint the stripes with alternating colors. Paint the narrow stripes with a tart, bright green. Then cool down the tartness by filling in the wide stripes with blue or purple. While the paint is still wet, remove the tape to reveal the white bands between the colors.

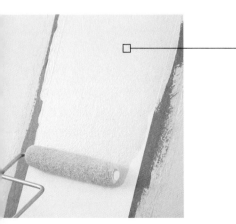

skill level: intermediate

The key to a good result is to measure, mark, and tape the wall before painting. Here are two ways to apply the tape.

Pencil Method: You'll need a good level with a straightedge and a hard-lead pencil that barely makes marks on the wall. Establish the first mark on the wall; draw a light line along the length of the level. Place the level above or below and extend the line. Repeat until the line is marked from ceiling to floor.

Gravity Method: Establish the placement of the tape with the first mark placed about 9 inches from the ceiling. Press the tape along the pencil mark. Then let the roll of tape drop to a point just above the floor. Allow it to swing into a natural resting position where it will hang perfectly straight. Carefully press the tape against the wall with the flat of your hand.

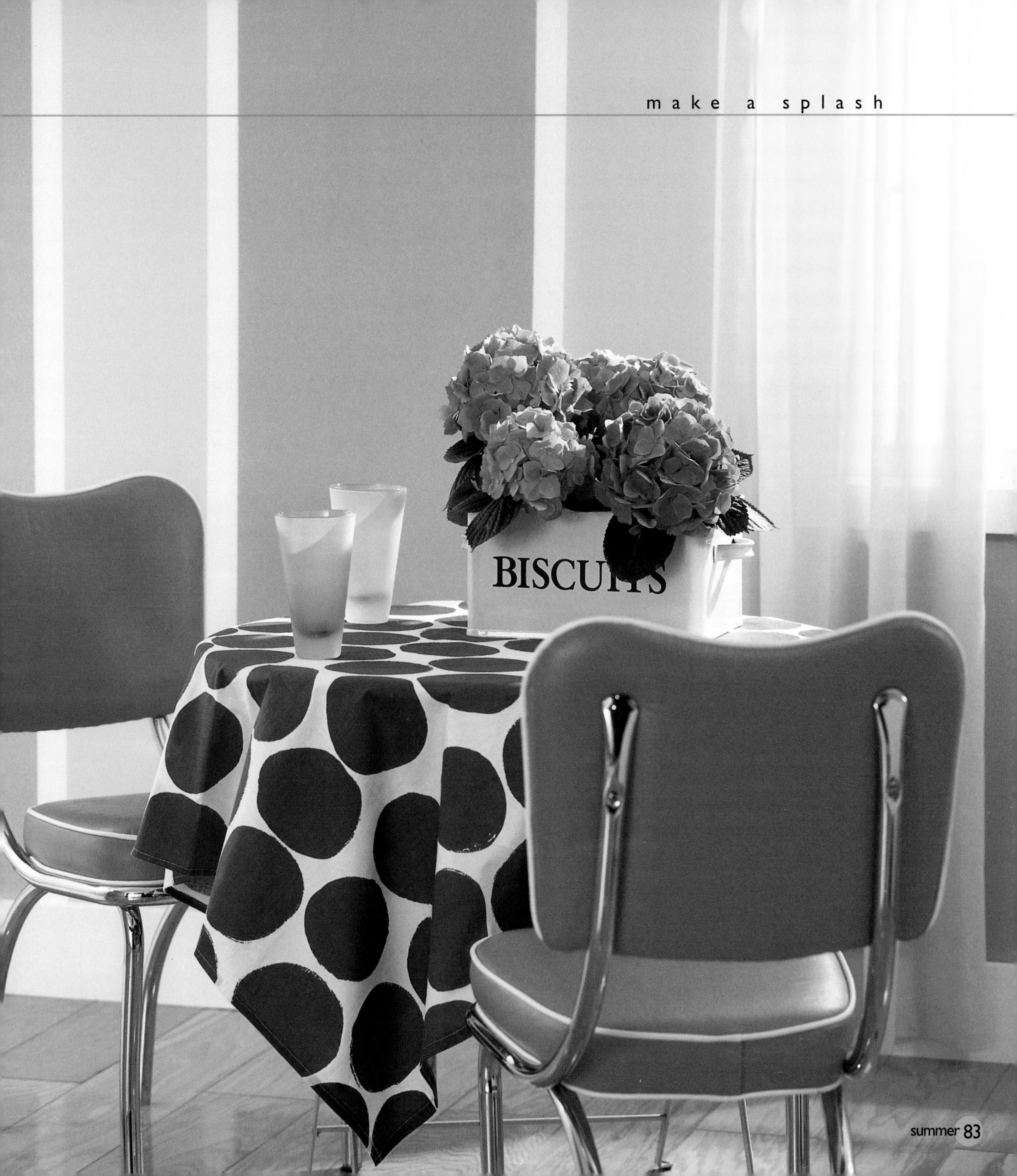
BISCUITS

molding makeover

Break up a long, tall wall with both vertical and horizontal strips of stock moldings you find on lumberyard shelves.

materials:

- **wall paint** (to coordinate with wallcovering)
- **wallcovering; wallcovering paste**
- **level; hard-lead pencil**
- **semigloss paint** (for molding)
- **$7/16 \times 1\frac{1}{4}$-inch undercap molding**
- **#6 finishing nails; wood glue; nail brads**
- **$7/16 \times 1\frac{3}{8}$-inch doorstop**
- **$1/4 \times 3/4$-inch screen molding**

Decorate the walls with wallcovering and paint. Begin by drawing the horizontal line using a level and a hard-lead pencil (the horizontal dividing line shown here fell 20 inches from the ceiling). Apply wallcovering below the line and paint above the line.

Paint all molding lengths before cutting them. For the horizontal molding, cut and fit the undercap to the wall. To attach it, nail through to studs (see tools and tips 101). Drill pilot holes for nails to prevent the moldings from splitting. Nail straight through the molding with finishing nails. Then glue the doorstop to the flat top of the undercap molding, holding it in place with a few small nails until the glue dries. For the vertical moldings, attach screen molding strips to the wall with wood glue and nail brads, spacing them 24 inches apart.

skill level: intermediate

tools and tips 101

To locate studs behind the covered surface, tap along the wall with a hammer and listen for solid thuds. Or use a commercial stud-finding device available in the tool section of home centers and hardware stores. Once you've found the first stud, measure off 16-inch intervals and you should find subsequent studs for nailing.

The spacing and lengths of these moldings can vary with the height of your ceilings, the length of your walls, and the positions of other architectural features in the room. As a general rule, a good point to position a horizontal dividing line is at one-fifth of the total height of the wall. Place the cosmetic vertical bands where they please your eye. Locate them wide apart for a relaxed look, close together for a busy one.

stamps of approval

Wake up a sleepy room with a splash of clear, uninhibited color.

Some of the color is painted on the walls; some of it is stamped on.

materials:

- flat white latex paint (base coat)
- carpenter's level; painter's tape; scissors; kraft paper
- red glaze (or color of your choice)
- stamping material (crafts store decorator blocks were used here)
- 48-ounce bottle of neutral glaze
- 2-ounce bottle of white glaze
- sponging mitt, sea sponge, or rag

Cover the walls with white paint; let dry. Using a level, mark a horizontal line on the wall 38 inches from the floor. Tape off the line with painter's tape and paint below the line with red glaze or glaze in the color of your choice. Enlarge patterns, *below,* to desired size on a copier. Cut out and trace the pattern onto the stamp materials. Cut out stamps. Coat one side of the stamp with white paint and press to red portion of the wall. Continue in a gridlike pattern. Repeat with red glaze and paisley stamp on the white wall. Let stamps dry.

Soften the hard-edge effect of the wall by mottling it with glaze. Mix all of the neutral glaze with all of the white glaze. Dampen the mitt or sea sponge and dip it into the glaze mixture. Blot the mitt or sponge onto kraft paper to remove any excess glaze. Gently blot glaze over the entire wall.

skill level: advanced

tools and tips 101

What is decorator's glaze? It's a water-based additive that gives paint translucency and allows you to layer colors for rich, dimensional surface treatments. Glazes come tinted or can be blended with acrylic or latex paints.

Glaze is a forgiving paint medium. If you don't like your results or make a mistake, you can immediately wipe off the glaze and start over. Keep wet rags on hand for quick cleanup.

Check out paint centers and home improvement stores for sponging mitts. You'll find them in the paint-finish tools section (located in the paint area), where you will also find handy tools for paint techniques, such as combing, ragging, rolling, and color-washing.

spring

Seasonal decorating in the dining room is really about what you bring to the table. For that, organize a closet of tabletop containers that you can pull out and use, then exchange for others when the season passes. To signal spring, look to the burgeoning garden, spring flower markets, or nurseries for fresh, newborn colors for your table. For vases, gather large greenhouse containers with light and airy qualities. Then cluster them on your table for between-meals centerpieces that will show off your newly picked garden blooms.

Set summer's table of simplicity with a centerpiece that doesn't need to be removed for meals. First, cover the table with a beach mat for a casual, fun twist to setting a table. Then set a tall, sand-filled florist's bucket to the left or right of the table center and stand five metal lantern hooks in the sand. Position the hooks so they hold the lanterns along the middle of the table. This centerpiece can stay for dinner because it's tall and spare and won't interrupt across-the-table views or dinner-table conversations.

You'll "autumnatically" turn to the season's edible abundance when fall comes around. Gather glass canning

jars, dried beans and peas from the grocery store, giant gourds, and warm-colored candles to blend togeth-

er in and out of a trug that takes center stage on the table. When it's time to serve dinner, lift the trug away

from the table and shift the separate canning jars together on the mat as a small centerpiece.

autumn

Make winter's tabletop simple and serene by covering it with a snowy-white tablecloth, frosted glass containers, mirror tile, and white candles. Keep the centerpiece narrow enough so it doesn't have to be removed for place settings. If you're planning a buffet, arrange large-size containers on a "runner" of mirror tile for a stunning winter party centerpiece.

winter

When the first leaves of autumn scatter in the urgent wind, celebrate the passing season by preparing for the next. Pull comforters from summer storage while the squirrels hide their acorns. Fluff up downy pillows and sink into natural comforts. Capture fleeting moments with a gathering of leaves and create decorating touches that will warm your nest.

autumn

You'll find an abundance of ideas in the chapter that follows.

color it cozy

Autumn's inviting palette is deep and comforting, especially during the colder seasons. It's also the easiest group of colors to use for decorating your home because earth tones are so familiar. Strong, sound, and reliable, autumn's reds, yellows, greens, and browns might mean a comfortable blend of mellow woods, rustic painted finishes, and nubby fabrics. Or it could be a scheme of redware, mustardy cabinets, sisal carpets, and soft stone walls. Whatever your style, this palette offers unlimited color choices that will support and ground your home and make it a place to which you'll gladly return each day.

Banister-back chairs, including one with a fish-tail top rail and original red paint, help make this living room one of the favorite places in the house. Beige upholstery surrounds an oval tavern table that also has original paint. Early American furniture may not be your style, but you can take color cues from colonial collections like this. Note how quietly patterned area rugs and pillows play against the plain surfaces of walls and upholstery.

Earth tones, generally low-key, deep, and dark, need the balance of lighter, midrange tones. By mixing cream-whites, mellow yellows, and pale golds into a scheme, you can lighten the mood of a room. Some folks enjoy living in a "cave" surrounded by dark, physical comforts; others need the sweet relief of open air in spite of the fact that they love to sink into upholstered, velvety chairs. It's a matter of selecting the light-and-dark scheme that fits your comfort level.

The clean-lined sofa, *opposite,* is a modern concession to comfort in this family room filled with antiques. Although the house is new, its owners set it back about 200 years with dark wainscoting, thick wooden ceiling beams, and deep-red wood stains. Red and brown quilt and curtain fabrics bring accent colors into the room.

Heart-shape sugar molds and checked fabrics decorate the wall in the breezeway; an easy-to-clean ceramic tile floor brings earthy warmth to the space.

Key to the decorating palette for the room, *left*, flat-styled Prior-Hamblin school portraits hang above this fireplace. To develop an autumn color scheme of your own, pull colors from a favorite painting or decorative object, such as a quilt or patterned fabric.

Neutral needn't be boring, thanks to a play of pattern and surface variation. The painted corner cupboard, rush-seated chairs, wooden treenware, and pottery supply the Early American dining room, *opposite*, with a lively collection of color and texture.

As they appear in nature, the laid-back shades of brown are best used at home in broken patterns and natural textures. Variegated wood grains on furniture, sandblasted wall surfaces, and faceted stones supply movement, light, and pattern in a room. They alleviate what otherwise might be a flat and lifeless scheme. For example, the flatly glazed ceramic tiles in the floor, *above*, are made lively by the linear pattern of light-colored grout lines that float between the chocolate-brown squares. Likewise, the dining room, *opposite*, is filled with pleasantly textured wood grains that shine through their painted surfaces. In addition, utilitarian tableware and handmade pottery, decorated with subtle patterns, supply the dining room with a rich diversity of textures.

Every color scheme needs a light source to bring it to life. Daylight that passes through windows is the best source because the purity of natural light allows colors to appear most true. Halogen lights are most like daylight, while most incandescent bulbs cast warm tones on surfaces. In an autumn scheme, avoid cool-toned fluorescent lighting.

A plain-colored linsey-woolsey coverlet spread over the reproduction bed, *left*, supplies restful neutral color and subtle texture. Soft lighting comes from the bedside table lamp created from an old jug and a corkscrew lamp kit (available in home improvement stores).

The 18th-century wall-mounted desk in the guest room, *above*, makes good use of leftover space at the end of the bed. The stenciled floor is new but painted in an authentic colonial pattern.

The leaves are falling. You can hear them whispering in the autumn wind, changing colors and directions, growing down instead of up. When they beg to come inside for one last blaze of glory, tuck them into wreaths and pots, pumpkins and frames. Here are eight ways to make the most of fall's abundance.

1 leaf wreath

To decorate a fall wreath, purchase a ready-made circle of wheat at a crafts supply store. Hang it on a wall where you'll see it often as you pass by. Gather turning leaves and slip their stems into the spaces between the wheat heads. Arrange in a spare manner so you don't lose the shapes of single leaves in an overcrowded mass. When the leaves fade, remove them and reuse the wreath another season.

gather a display

candle gourd

Turn a gourd into a candleholder by first cutting off the top. Then, to insert a 3-inch-diameter candle, hollow out the center of the gourd with a knife and an ice cream scoop. Set the candle in the hollow and secure it in place with florist's clay. Keeping the decorations well away from the wick, dress the cut edge of the gourd with leaves, berries, and pods. And remember: Never leave a lighted candle unattended.

3 windfall hangings

Suspend leaves on beaded silk cords. First, purchase red, gold, and orange glass beads and lengths of shiny cording from fabric and crafts supply stores. Then knot the cord ends and thread two beads on each cord; slip leaf stems through the knots and beads. Hang the leaves in front of a window where you can enjoy the light as it illuminates the leaves' weblike structures.

4 works of art

Press and display your favorite fallen leaves. **Pull on a sweater and head outdoors on a leaf-collecting expedition.** When you return, place the leaves between the pages of a book. Allow the leaves to flatten and dry for a few days. Then slip the best specimens between the panes of glass-backed frames over pinked or torn mats of handmade paper.

5 nesting bowls

Stack a pair of wooden bowls for height and dimension. Then fill the top bowl with apples. Sprinkle the apples with leaves as if the bowl has just arrived from orchard picking. For a graceful arch over the display area, set a large urn nearby and allow maple branches to spill from the neck of the urn over the bowls.

apple tart

Center a candle in a bowl of apples to shed new light on an old classic. Nestle a stocky candle in the middle of a simple glass salad or punch bowl, then fill around it with small fruits. There's no need to purchase a tall, expensive candle; choose a short one and elevate it on a candlestand or aluminum can. Then hide the stand or can with apples.

harvest centerpiece

Pull together market produce for a colorful celebration of the season. Arrange the round shapes of blood oranges, pears, and kumquats on a cake plate and in berry boxes. For whimsical flower vases, hollow out small pumpkins or squash with a kitchen knife or apple corer. Fill the hollows with water and insert flower stems in a pleasing arrangement.

8
baskets of bounty

Arrange miniature baskets in a tray or box to create an edible display of orchard gatherings and kitchen treats. To find suitable containers, venture into country stores and marketplaces. Look for garden flats, trays with sides, even miniature carts with wheels. Here, the display tray is a vintage toy wagon that's pulled behind wooden horses. It serves as a tabletop centerpiece from early fall through the holiday season, and guests are invited to indulge in its ever-changing contents. The tiny baskets were found at antiques shops in the miniatures sections and on doll and toy shelves.

feather
your nest

Like birds, we weave together the comforts of home. It's instinctive. When summer's end signals that fall decorating flurry, go with the flow. You may get the urge to bake pies, stack firewood, or warm your bed with quilts. Decorate with pumpkins—it's natural. Gather the family for a celebration and plan a feast for the eyes as well as the appetite. The table, *opposite,* is an example of decorating zeal. Moving the table to the fireside just for the occasion creates intimacy and a festive mood.

Light candles if you don't have a fireplace. The effect of any flame, large or small, is the same. It symbolizes warmth and security, peace and comfort. Gather candles on a tray to carry to a side table when a sudden need to celebrate turns up. Buy candlestands for large signature candles that work as fireside-like focal points near a seating group. Keep a stash of candles in a closet for special occasions.

Gather furniture together in groups. It will encourage conversation, storytelling, and reconnecting. Be sure that each seat has a table surface nearby for lamps, books, and drinking glasses. Side tables, sofa tables, and coffee tables are the standards for keeping you and your family comfortable, but you can create unique (and more interesting) chairside tables from pieces of salvage. Plant stands, stacked crates, antique carts, and footstools can also serve as tables to keep armchair comforts within easy reach.

For fall, layer summer's sheer window treatment with greenery. After all, outdoor plants like to come in for the cold season too. The benefits? That safe, cozy-up feeling you get from sitting under the shade of a tree; an easy way to soften a window treatment; and more fresh air to breathe when you're shut inside.

Pool your resources. For quiet dinners, a cluster of candles is more romantic than one or two tapers. Choose a variety of shapes and sizes in colors that complement the time of year. Fill bookcases with generous baskets to hold linens and silver, candles and holders, and your stash of seasonal tabletop decorations.

Rearrange furniture. While you may not have an open-plan living space, such as the one *at right*, a room arrangement change of your own will give you a fresh outlook. Check the room-arranging primer in the back of this book for ideas to fit your rooms. In the process, remove useless, unappealing objects from your home and replace them with items that warm your heart.

summer

autumn

To escape a decorating rut, rearrange a room. For this homeowner, it means flopping the great-room arrangement. Part of the year, the seating group faces the fireplace and the dining room is set at the other end of the open-plan space. Come autumn (and fall cleaning), the living and dining areas change places and a fresh perspective is gained.

Summer's simplified dining room may be left unused if you dine alfresco most of the season. But when it's time to come inside for warmth in the fall, you'll want to soften summer's clean, crisp edges.

summer

autumn

Awaken the senses with a tabletop display. Successful decorating appeals to the eyes and to the other four senses as well. An easy place to engage the senses is in the dining room, where everyone gathers around a large table. The tabletop is a perfect platform for a centerpiece of beautiful and touchable objects that can be appreciated between and during meals. Mix items of various textures, making sure to include some with rough and smooth surfaces, some with hard and soft. For the sense of sound, play soft music, hang wind chimes, or open windows to let in nature's noises. Arrange fresh flowers or lightly scented candles to tantalize the sense of smell. Tease taste palates with a generous plate of fruit or a bowl of candy.

Slip upholstered chair cozies over summer's bare-boned dining room seats. Here, toile covers warm the backs of Windsor dining chairs and echo the room's red wall color. You can buy standard chair coverings ready-made from home furnishings stores and catalogs. To fit special chairs, hire a seamstress. Or, to sew your own, purchase dressmaker patterns at a fabric store. You'll find a wide selection in the home decorating sections of pattern books.

For friendly, familiar faces, accent tabletops with representations of nature's creatures. In this display, ceramic birds and carved sheep bring the outdoors in with the change of season. If birds and sheep don't appeal to you, incorporate natural objects that do.

Lay fabric on tabletops to soften summer's stripped-down look. The color and weave of fabric work naturally to invite indoor dining once the season of dining alfresco is spent. For a light look, choose fine, white weaves; for a rich, autumn feeling, select nubby, coarse weaves in warm colors.

Wrap a seating group with a fencelike floor screen that gives the room a sense of protection or a psychological shield from the elements. Decoratively, the screen adds a layer to summer's simple window treatment and pulls the seating pieces together. To make the freestanding screen, buy a ready-made fence panel from a lumberyard and cut it into thirds. Hinge the sections together to fold and stand on the floor in a zigzagging position.

Keep windows lightly covered so the sunshine continues to come inside. Nothing darkens a room's attitude like a lack of light, and autumn is no time to shun the sun. Sheer white window coverings work best year-round to let in light and soften window glass. They also provide good underpinnings for decorative window treatments.

Add pattern with fabric. A room with one fabric pattern has a sophisticated, cool look; more patterns make a room feel casual and cozy. To mix patterns easily, stay with one color, such as red, and add a stripe or a mini-pattern that coordinates with the main print.

Re-cover an old chair for more cushioned comfort. You can order fabric through an upholsterer or at a fabric store that carries fabrics to coordinate with your existing upholstery.

summer

A sitting room in summer feels cool with fewer furnishings, and a less-is-more decorating theory keeps the sticky season at bay. When autumn arrives and you feel decorating changes in the wind, accommodate your wish for warmth by adding more.

autumn

paint it
comfortable

color combing

Create this rustic finish with a window-washing squeegee and wall comb. You'll find these paint-finish tools at your paint retailer.

materials:

- satin or semigloss acrylic paints in two closely related shades
- painter's tape
- decorator's wall glaze
- paint tray and roller
- squeegee with ¼-inch notches
- wall comb

Cover the walls with the darker shade of paint; let dry. Tape off a 4-foot-square section of wall. Mix 5 parts glaze with 1 part of the lighter shade of paint. Roll the glaze mixture on the taped-off section. While the glaze is still wet, start at the top of the section and pull the squeegee down the wall, making vertical stripes. Repeat across the glazed section, working quickly. Remove the painter's tape. Repeat these steps across the wall. In subsequent sections, paint over the wet edge and tape the dry edges only. Let the paint dry at least six hours.

Tape off a 4-foot-square section of wall. Roll the glaze mixture over the section.

Starting at the top of the section, comb horizontally through the glaze. Repeat, working quickly down the wall. Remove the painter's tape. Repeat across the wall, working in 4-foot-square sections.

skill level: intermediate

Before painting your walls with a decorative finish, try the technique on foam-core board. Aside from the painting practice, you'll have a sample to post on the wall before making a commitment.

The squeegee used in this technique and purchased at the paint store is large and works best on flat, open walls. It doesn't fit into tight spaces. To solve this problem, create a pint-size squeegee: Use a sharp crafts knife to cut notches into a small window-washing squeegee to match the notches in the larger one.

Glaze is a forgiving paint medium. If you don't like your results or make a mistake, you can immediately wipe off the glaze and start over. Keep wet rags on hand for quick cleanup.

leaf stenciling

This technique is a reverse stencil. You cut a shape from acetate and, rather than discarding the cutout, use the shape as your stencil.

materials:

- ■ fern, philodendron, and geranium leaves
- ■ clear or opaque stencil acetate
- ■ fine-tip permanent marking pen; crafts knife
- ■ interior latex paints in two related colors (one for background, one for leaves)
- ■ neutral decorator's wall glaze
- ■ quick-release painter's tape; paint tray; stencil roller
- ■ clean, lint-free rags; cutting mat

Choose a few leaves with interesting shapes and textures. Press them between books for a day or two to flatten. Photocopy the flat, dry leaves. Trace the patterns onto stencil acetate using a fine-tip permanent marking pen. Using a crafts knife with a new blade and working on a cutting mat, cut out the leaf patterns. Paint the background color on the wall and let it dry overnight.

Mix 3 parts wall glaze with 1 part of the leaf paint. Pour a small amount of the tinted glaze into a paint tray. Working from the top of the wall down, hold one stencil or pressed leaf on the wall at a time with your fingertips. Use a stencil roller to roll the glaze over the stencil. Apply six or seven more leaves in this manner, randomly placing and overlapping them as you wish.

Using a slightly damp rag, dab and smudge stenciled images to eliminate harsh edges and to camouflage the stops and starts.

skill level: advanced

You can also use real pressed leaves as your stencil; however, you'll want to have several of each leaf type on hand because the leaves break easily. Aside from the fern, philodendron, and geranium leaves used here, other striking options include buckeye, locust, oak, and maple leaves.

When you paint the background color on the wall, protect the moldings and ceiling where they meet the wall with quick-release painter's tape, available at paint supply stores. Press the tape firmly in place to prevent paint from seeping under it.

A cutting mat is a valuable tool whether you're cutting fabric, paper, or acetate. You'll find small and large sizes at art supply, fabric, and crafts supply stores.

discover
treasure

Buy new life for an old castoff. **Flea markets and secondhand stores are perfect places to find pieces that will add dimension to your decorating style and more storage to your home. For example, this weathered plant stand came indoors to serve as a nightstand and bookcase while enjoying an easier life under a pool of warm light.**

create

SIMPLIFY YOUR LIFE · ELAINE ST. JAMES

The Art of Doing Nothing

A KISS IS JUST A KISS · YELLES · HARMONY BOOKS

The Ribbon: A Gift of Remembrance · Hugh Storey · CHRONICLE BOOKS

Web·Life

GRIMM'S COMPLETE
FAIRY TALES

ANGELS
AN ENDANGERED SPECIES   MALCOLM GODWIN

Roads to Paradise
Reading the Lives of the Early Saints

The MYSTICAL MARRIAGE · GERHARD WEHR

NEW TESTAMENT & PSALMS

MONICA'S STORY   ANDREW MORTON

POPE JOHN XXIII · LAZZARINI

MOTHER TERESA   MY OWN WORDS

bedside bookcase

2 blanket box

Combine unrelated items to create new storage. Purchase large crates for small amounts of cash and turn them into valuable stashes for big items, such as blankets, quilts, and pillows. To give a crate a visual and practical lift from the floor, set it on a pair of well-used camp stools.

3 book stack

Build a bookcase from wooden boxes. Set bigger boxes on the bottom and smaller ones on top. In no time, you'll have a pyramid to house your favorite reads. This stack is small, but consider building a larger one. Place same-size boxes side by side as a bottom tier or bookshelf, several more like-size boxes for a middle tier, and smaller boxes for a top tier.

4 tool totes

Reorganize and recycle. Once a toolbox, always a toolbox—but not always toting the same old things. Store kitchen tools in a shoe-polishing kit. Cut string from a wood shop carrier. Gather tableware in a six-pack carton.

5 stacking stool

Give an old stool new reasons to work. Freshen it first with a new coat of paint. Then seat a plant on top and stack a tower of plates on the support rails below.

6
towel bins

7
rake rack

Rummage through antiques shops for stylish ways to store towels. The two old-fashioned discoveries *above* have found new-fashioned usefulness. Once used as bins in a hardware store, the open shelves *at left* now keep stacks of towels ready for service. To make the kitchen towel rack, *right*, purchase an old-time wooden rake, cut the handle to a shorter length, and drill a hole through the end of the handle. Hang the rake from a hook on the wall or from a peg rack.

8
hooked on salvage

To give a piece of yesterday's architectural salvage a useful purpose for today, buy sturdy, old-looking wire hooks from a hardware store. Attach the hooks on the plain, lower edge of a pediment or decorative arch to turn it into a hanging place for robes, towels, or clothing. Look for salvage pieces with rustic finishes and carvings to complement modern-day fabric textures.

BARBIZON-PLAZA
HOTEL
NEW YORK CITY

9 open-door store

Leave the door open on a small cupboard to store bath necessities on open shelves. Decorate the back of the door and top of the cupboard with salt-water souvenirs. To extend the usefulness of the storage unit, add a shelf with hooks beneath the cupboard. You'll create a unit of storage that's both practical and a stylish focal point in the room.

10 basket access

Set secondhand baskets in strategic places. Easy to access, attractive, and affordable, they provide storage space with style. Use baskets in your entry to catch bills and mail, in the bath to store toiletries, or in an office to hold extra paper. Combine different shapes, sizes, textures, and materials to multiply the storage space and make a style statement.

materials:

- 2½ yards of 54-inch-wide solid-color velvet fabric
- 2½ yards of 54-inch-wide damask patterned velvet fabric
- sewing thread
- 2 tension rods to fit door opening
- upholstery cord tiebacks; hooks

For a standard 7-foot-high door opening, hem the long sides of each panel. On the top of each panel, sew 2-inch-wide rod pockets. Slip the tension rods through the rod pockets and temporarily hang the panels in the doorway to measure the correct hem lengths. Remove the rods and hem the bottoms of the panels with 3-inch-wide hems.

Shir the panels back onto the rods and fasten the rods, one in front of the other, in the door opening.

Slip the panels through the loops of the tiebacks and tie the cords to hooks fastened in the door frame.

skill level: intermediate

door drape

nourish
a view

silk panels

materials:

- 2½ yards of 50-inch-wide gold silk fabric (for one panel)
- silk upholstery cording
- gold sewing thread
- bamboo curtain rod

For a standard 84-inch panel, press under all edges ½ inch. Turn under sides and bottom an additional 2½ inches. Press and hem the three edges by hand or by machine. Turn under the top edge ½ inch; press and hem it.

Whipstitch silk upholstery cording across the top of the panel, creating 5-inch-long loops for hanging at equal intervals.

Slip the hanging loops over a bamboo curtain rod.

skill level: beginner

clip curtains

materials:

- two 55-inch × 100-inch rectangular tablecloths
- clip curtain rings
- curtain rod and brackets

Leaving the border intact at the bottom and along the sides, cut each tablecloth to 84½ inches long. The excess fabric will be 15-inch-long valances.

Lay one panel flat, right side down. Place a valance on top of it, right side down and upper edges matching. Pin and sew along the top edge, using ½-inch seam allowances. Flip the valance to the right side of the panel; press. Topstitch through all layers ½ inch from the seam. Repeat for the other panel.

Attach curtain rings to the top edge of each panel and slip the rings over the curtain rod.

skill level: intermediate

materials:

- 8 yards of 48-inch-wide white damask lace
- serger sewing machine
- silver eyelets; eyelet tool
- wire curtain cable; brackets
- lightweight silver metallic cord

Cut the lace into four 2-yard panels. To hem, serge all raw edges of the panels.

Using the eyelet tool, punch silver eyelets into the top of each panel, placing them about 7 inches apart and about 1½ inches from the top edge.

Hang the curtain cable from the ceiling following the package instructions. Run a 2-yard length of silver cord through each eyelet and slip the cord over the cable. Position the lace panel about 2 inches from the floor by pulling the cord up and tying the ends of the cord on the back side of the curtain near the eyelet. Pull the panels to each side of the window.

skill level: intermediate

lace curtain

spring

Nothing expresses seasonal change like color. Think spring with barely-there pastels and wake up to pale sunshine, white flowers from the garden, and easy-on-the-eye fabrics. White sheets and pillowcases work well in spring for a light look, and sheer window treatments invite the sun inside. But here's a notable change to make: Exchange winter's heavy comforter for a lightweight summer one. Slip a fresh-colored cover over the comforter and toss it lightly over the sheets for a simple, low-maintenance bed.

summer

Color your bedroom cool for summer. When evenings warm to unbearable temperatures, light blues and whites seem cooler to the eye than reds, oranges, and browns. Keep most of your bedding white and light by storing the duvet and covering the bed with a simple matelassé spread. Toss on a pair of breezy, blue patterned pillowcases and give your nightstand small, hot shots of purples and poppy orange to remind yourself that summer (in reality) is made up of sizzling color, hot sun, and fully blooming flowers.

Pull out an extra quilt when evenings begin to cool. It's best if it's a blend of autumn hues, all toasty-warm and rich with the colors of ripening pumpkins, apples, and plums. In nature's season of abundance, it's time to splurge on color for your bed. Exchange your usual white sheets for linens in red, rust, and gold. Layer on textured throws of lavender or peach. Get out your photo albums for warm memories, or read in bed.

autumn

Winter whites cover a bed's dark shapes the way snow blankets a landscape of barren trees. Sink into the layers of winter with lavender and white linens, a fluffy feather bed, a winter-weight duvet, and a transparent bedcovering of icy voile. If you keep colors light in winter, your spirit will maintain its lightness longer during the stretches of time that the sun takes leave. Keep evergreens on your nightstand to remind you that not all things grow down and brown in winter.

winter

A wondrous kind of quiet comes with feathery layers of new snow. Falling softly in fat, hypnotic flakes, the season's first blanket of white settles lightly over the landscape like a down-filled comforter. Before long, you feel the urge to ready your rooms for a long winter's nap or to re-energize them with spirit-lifting decorating ideas that thrive in the coldest of seasons.

winter

urn the pages for dozens of ways to winterize your home.

color it calm

Winter's palette falls from the sky, its colors diffused by clouds and altered by rain and snow. While some people are less than enthusiastic about the grayed-down hues of the coldest season, others find them as comfortable and reassuring as the season that brings them. They're the colors of dormancy and suspension of activity, a temporary cessation from external affairs. Sound like home? When home is a place of retreat and return from the outside world of activity, neutralized colors are the colors for you. They'll heal and content you, calm and revitalize your spirits, and prepare you for the next day's engagements.

Light, fresh, and uncomplicated, fireside seating gathers around a marble fireplace and coffee table colored in stone-solid hues. Neutral fabrics of varying whites unify old and new upholstered pieces, making them seem like part of the same furniture family. Black stain on the old oak floor puts a dramatic and reassuring foundation under the neutral furnishings while tying everything to the black walls of the adjacent dining room.

For many, a neutral color scheme is either a first choice or a last resort. In both cases, the biggest decorating risk is over-neutralizing. The antidote to color monotony is threefold: First, use not just one color but many shades of the same color. Second, compensate for the lack of strong color by emphasizing surface textures, shapes, and dimension. And, last, undergird your rooms with a few dark contrasts to give them solid ground to stand on.

This intimate seating area in the living room, *opposite,* centers on a white-and-gold tea table. Quietly patterned and textured upholstery emphasizes the shapes and contours of the seating pieces and provides a tactile quality often missing in one-color rooms.

Black walls provide neutral ground in the dining room, *right,* putting the furniture into a contemporary context. Although the dining and living rooms are at opposite ends of the color spectrum, the dark-stained floor is the common bond.

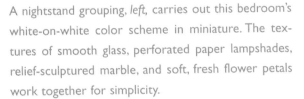

A nightstand grouping, *left*, carries out this bedroom's white-on-white color scheme in miniature. The textures of smooth glass, perforated paper lampshades, relief-sculptured marble, and soft, fresh flower petals work together for simplicity.

As soothing and therapeutic as the living room, the winter whites of the bedroom, *opposite*, stress texture by way of plantation shutters, a tufted duvet, a quilted bed skirt, and artwork that's placed high and low to give dimension to what otherwise might be an imposing solid wall of taupe. Clustered together, the frames form a kind of unit or collage. The gilded sunburst mirror provides a focal point and visual relief from the squares and rectangles of the rest of the grouping.

In elementary school, everyone learns that white is the absence of color. However, in nature, white embraces a rainbow of subtle hues, from the palest of pinks and lavenders to tints of blue, green, and gray. Avalon Beige, Dusting Powder Pink, Irish Cream, Linen Cloth, and Frosted Glass are a few color names that conjure up the varied essences of white. To banish the chill of pure, cold whites, such as Crushed Ice or Blizzard, choose whites that whisper of warmer days. Candleglow, Sugarplum, Drowsy Lavender, and Paper Moon have connotations of softness and comfort rather than of a cold drift of snow.

Silence is that enchanted place where the room empties of chatter, time stands still, and the landscape expands like the morning after a snowfall. Fish swim idly under the river's ice, and flowers sleep beneath cool blankets of white. In the quiet of winter's silence, you can hear the still, small voice of your decorating soul softening in repose.

Lawn and deck chairs, *opposite,* may stay out all winter once the first blanket of snow falls. Snowflakes, gathering on their backs and seats, invite wonderland sitting on softly contoured snow pads and pillows.

White's mystical nature plays out well in arrangements of classic pieces. Like the snowy scene, the arrangement, *above,* employs dark, structural lines to define large expanses of white. Accents of wine red energize the composition.

warm up

Short days and long nights leave more hours for home entertainment of the decorating kind. When the cold winds blow from the north, settle in for the duration and consider the next few pages. You'll find six candle and lighting ideas that will get you filling your home with that close-to-the-fire feeling.

1 lightning rod candlestands

Set slender, tapered candles upside down in the disk holes of antique lightning rod brackets for a surprising, eclectic way to light a wide stair or entry. The long tapers at the tops of the candles make the candle fitting easy and safe. Trim away some of the wax at the bottoms of the candles to expose the wicks. Once the candles are set, decorate the wire stands with long lengths of wide satin ribbon that drop gracefully to the floor.

2 entry table

Welcome family home with warmth when the weather is cold and wet.

Whether your entry is large enough to hold a significant table or so small that you can barely squeeze in a classic pediment, there's always room for a decorative gesture. Add a glimmer of candlelight, a sparkling mirror, or a fresh flower to oppose the outdoor chill.

3 lanterns alight

Collect old-fashioned oil lanterns to light the way down a long hall or to illuminate a dark corner. Keep a color scheme in mind as you acquire the lanterns, so the look is unified. For example, this collection is centered on lanterns with bodies and bases of clear glass and white marble, milk glass, or china. Choose a color scheme that suits your decor and begin the hunt.

4 nest of lights

Turn a grapevine wreath into a light ring by spray-painting it white. When it's dry, place the ring on a side table where it will be a bright focal point in a gathering room. Wind strings of white-wired, miniature holiday lights around the grapevine ring and find an inconspicuous electrical outlet on the wall in the room. Then center a crystal punch bowl in the space inside the ring and fill the bowl with white, silver, and crystal ball ornaments originally intended for the tree.

5 beaded bobeche

String colored-glass beads on 20-gauge silver bead wire. To space the beads along the wire, kink the wire by wrapping it once around a round-nose pliers. You'll find beads and wire in the jewelry section of crafts supply stores.

6 vase candleholders

Center tall candles in identical glass vases. Hold the candles with one hand while you fill the vases one-third full with white sea glass. This gives the look of ice without the melting.

snuggle in

Wrap a room in white if you prefer the pristine qualities of gently falling snow to the traditional dark colors often used for winter decorating. Few things are more perfectly serene. Frost windows with filmy sheers to keep the light coming in despite cloudy days. Marbleized walls solidify the white color scheme and keep it from disappearing into a snowstorm. If you like the effect of marble as a year-round backdrop, hire a painter to marbleize the walls for you, or do them yourself with a kit purchased at a crafts supply store.

Place cream-white, textured upholstery pieces in a face-to-face arrangement around a tree. When the holiday passes, remove the tree, angle the seating pieces into a winged arrangement for a cozier feel, and place an off-white, textured area rug on the floor to define the chat room. Then move a tea table into the center of the seating group for the rest of the season.

Perhaps you can't hibernate, but you can take the chill off with warm colors, rich textures, and furniture pieces that invite nestling in. To make your favorite room especially snug this winter, paint a wall, add golden lamplight, or simply rearrange the furniture.

Take slick new windows back to cozier times, stylewise, with a plate rail that includes pegs for curtain hanging. Here the two rails visually knit together a corner and balance the height of the cupboard. For simple curtains to hang from the pegs, sew loops along the tops of fabric panels that have been lined for warmth. Then hook the loops over the pegs as desired (you can easily change them to close off the window completely or stack the loops to gather the curtains at the sides of the window). For an open, spacious look in spring and summer, simply remove the panels from the window and rearrange accessories on the ledges to suit the season.

Turn a corner into an irresistible dining nook with a ready-made booth. The paneled design of the booth adds instant architecture, while plump cushions and quilts lend softness to the seats. Once the stationary pieces are set, mix the styles of movable seating around the rest of the table. Clean-lined classics, such as benches, bow-back Windsors, or a web-seated Shaker high chair, blend easily with the simple lines of the booth. For the focal-point impact of a warm fireplace, slide in a tall china cupboard with interior lights and a back covered with reflective glass. The cupboard, set at an angle, reflects the cozy view and heats up the room's snuggle-in factor.

Use prepasted wallcoverings and paint colors with a classic, no-color attitude that can flow with the change of the seasons. Basic whites with small amounts of black or other neutral colors work easily for winter's get-cozy times, as well as for spring and summer's more open, freewheeling arrangements.

Connect your surroundings to the past with accessories that tell stories. Punched-tin lights and utilitarian implements with well-worn finishes add dimension to your gather-round-the-table decorating theme.

When the view at the window is frosted over, a painted wall around glass panes can take you back to long-ago seasons or send you dreaming into the future. To decorate a wall, hire an artist. Or do it yourself with a stencil kit you choose at a crafts supply store.

Build a cozy nook for sleeping in. This cottage getaway, built under the eaves, is basically an extended window seat framed by an interior window to the room. A wall of beaded-board wainscoting surrounds it all. Inside the nook, walls are sponged an antique cream, then painted with a tree mural that arches over the window.

Furnish a privacy nest with a wall sconce that provides light for reading, and add recessed bookshelves to hold plenty of bedtime stories. Pad the mattress with quilted textures and layer on blankets of fleece or velvet. Surround the opening with hardy green plants that can survive the low lights of winter and little attention from you. After all, you'll be occupied with more important matters, such as reading a good book or taking a nap.

Add nookside comforts by selecting furniture pieces that lend style and service to the hideaway's interior. This antique chair works as a bedside coffee table. If you build a nook raised in a room, you may need a stool or ladder for entry. Bed curtains hung in the window opening would add warmth, and a shelf built inside the nook would serve as a bedside table or bookshelf.

Store extra linens and blankets out of sight in the cabinets built at the base of the berth.

revitalize with
color

painted floor

A Swedish-inspired oval garland of leaves and branches can be a lighter way to define floor space than laying down a heavy rug.

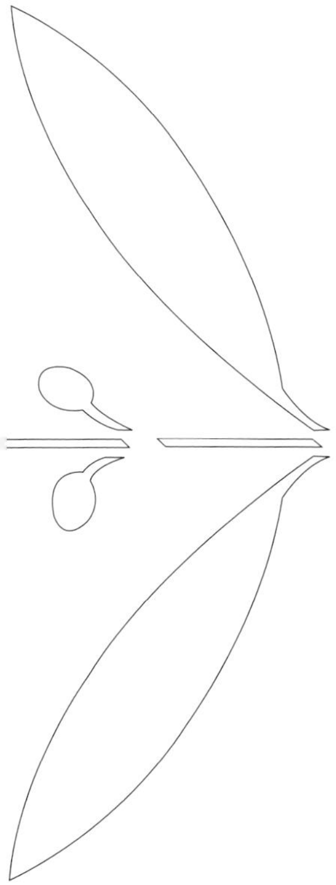

materials:

- high-quality flat latex white floor paint
- pad-style paint applicator
- lint-free cloths; emery paper; transparent tape
- blank stencil plastic; sharp crafts knife
- hard-lead pencil or water-erasable sewing marker
- blue stencil paint (available in crafts supply stores)
- clear varnish

To begin, enlarge the leaf pattern, *left*, to the desired size. Cut the pattern from the blank stencil plastic and prepare the floor surface. See tools and tips 101 for hints for accomplishing all three.

To paint the base coat on the floor, use a pad-style applicator. Apply a coat of high-quality flat latex paint. Then repeat with two more coats, allowing sufficient drying time between steps. This will vary with humidity and air circulation and could take several days.

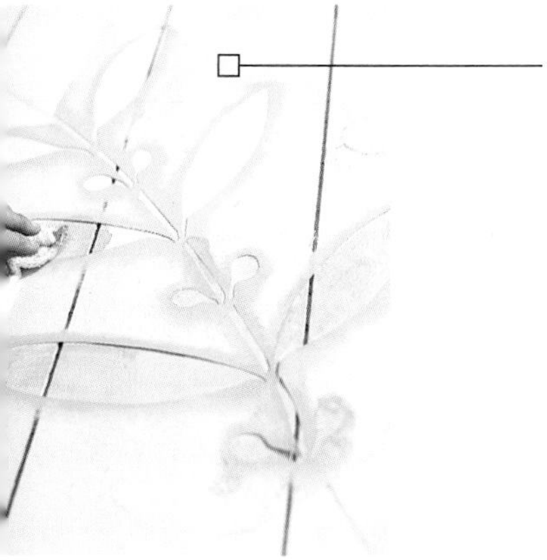

To apply the decorative design, mark the floor with a circle or oval in the desired size, using a hard lead pencil or sewing marker. Align the stencil with the line you've drawn on the floor. Dip a lint-free cloth into blue paint, then blot it onto paper to remove most of the paint. Gently press the cloth to the floor through the stencil opening. Remove the stencil and move it to the next position. After the completed stenciled design dries, cover the floor with one or more coats of varnish.

skill level: intermediate

tools and tips 101

To enlarge the design, *left*, take the pattern on this page to a copy center and ask to have the design enlarged to your desired overall dimensions (this one measures about 7 inches high and 16 inches wide). For a small rug, half the size of the one shown here, ask for an enlargement about 3½ inches high and 8 inches wide.

To prepare a stencil, transfer the design to blank plastic. Tape the stencil to a piece of glass or self-healing mat. Cut out the design with a sharp crafts knife. Smooth any rough edges with emery paper and tape over any stray cuts with transparent tape.

To prepare the floor, remove old varnish or wax, fill in gouges with paintable wood filler, and sand the floor. Wipe with a tack cloth, then scrub it with a liquid floor cleaner.

picture gallery

Enliven a blank wall with small photos framed by picture mats of exaggerated size. Cut them from mat board in winter colors.

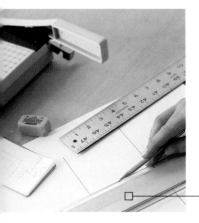

materials:

- 20-inch × 30-inch mat boards
- large paper cutter or utility knife and straightedge
- T-square
- ruler
- pencil with eraser
- mat cutter with guide rail

Cut the outside edges of the mat the same size as your frame inset. Use a large paper cutter or a sharp utility knife and a straightedge.

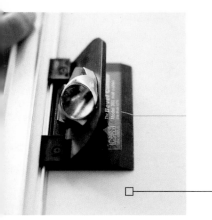

Measure and mark the picture opening. To plan the measurements, place the image at the center on the back of the mat. With a ruler, measure equal distances from the four edges of the image to the four edges of the mat. Subtract an inch or so from the top measurement and add it to the bottom (artwork positioned slightly above center appears more balanced when it is viewed from a distance). Place the T-square against the edge of the mat to make sure your lines are square and, with the ruler, measure and mark the opening on the back of the mat with a pencil.

Make the cuts and remove the center rectangle. See tools and tips 101, right, for how to use a mat cutter. If you follow the instructions for operating the mat cutter precisely, the center rectangle should lift out smoothly. Place the picture over the opening and fasten it onto the back of the mat with white art tape.

skill level: advanced

tools and tips 101

To use a mat cutter, follow the instructions that come with it. They will read something like this: Set the cutter for the beveled opening position. Place mat in the cutter, color side down. Slide it under the guide rail and against the mat guide. Line up the marked line with the right edge of the guide rail. Position the mat cutter so the silver indicator line aligns with the bottom intersecting pencil line. Hold downward pressure on the rail with your left hand and place your right thumb on the blade holder's thumb divot. Plunge the blade into the mat. Lower the heel of your hand behind the cutting head for maximum leverage. Slide the cutter away from you until it intersects with the upper line; don't pass the line. Pull the blade holder into the up position to remove it from the mat. Rotate the mat and repeat for the remaining sides.

tie-dyed fabrics

Color white cotton fabrics with grocery-store dyes to liven up your bedding inventory. Or hang your newly dyed panels at a window.

materials:

- **2 packages of fabric dye** (we used one kelly green and one teal package of RIT dye)
- **6 yards of white 100% cotton fabric**
- **1 bag of size 33 rubber bands**
- **2 cups salt; chlorine bleach**
- **4-gallon enamel pot**
- **latex gloves**

To prepare the fabric, wash and dry it in a regular wash cycle. Cut it into 2½-yard pieces. For striped fabric, gather the fabric lengthwise loosely into a long tube. Wrap rubber bands around the tube, placing them in bunches about 2 to 3 inches apart. In each bunch, use three to five rubber bands, wrapping them each three times around the fabric. The fabric will look like a segmented rope. For dotted fabric, spread the fabric out, then pinch it into bunches about 4 inches apart, wrapping rubber bands around each pinched bunch five times. Place four bunches horizontally and seven vertically.

Prepare dye according to package instructions. *Note:* Be sure to wear latex gloves while handling dye.

Dye the fabric using one of the methods described in tools and tips 101, right. Remove the rubber bands, rinse the fabric, and let it air-dry. Stitch into pillowcases using a purchased pillowcase as a pattern, or purchase a pattern from a fabric store.

skill level: beginner

tools and tips 101

For the washing machine dyeing method, fill the washer with 9 gallons (use low wash cycle) of hot water. Open the lid and mix the dye and salt mixture into the wash water. Run cold water over the fabric and place it in the washing machine. Run the cycle set for hot wash and cold rinse. Remove the fabric and clean washer with 1 cup of bleach in a wash cycle.

For the stove-top method, place 3 gallons of water in a large pot on the stove. Add the dye and stir. Wet the fabric with hot water and add to the pot. Bring dye bath to a simmer. Stir constantly until desired color is reached (up to 30 minutes). Turn off the stove and remove the fabric. Rinse fabric in warm water, then gradually cool the water until the water runs clear. Clean the pot immediately with bleach to avoid staining.

soothe
your senses

Few things have the power to renew the spirit like a long soak in a hot bath. Escape to a spa right at home by decorating a tub area with magical touches that will take you away. Hang a floor-to-ceiling length of white cotton voile as a privacy screen for your bath. A shower curtain rod, fastened close to the ceiling, works to hang the fabric panel with narrow ribbons through grommeted holes. Add a small fold-up chair to serve as a tubside caddy, light votive candles safely away from the curtain, and slip into sultry waters.

Conjure the feeling of an invigorating bath in the midst of snowy woods. Do-it-yourself beaded-board and wood flooring kits are an easy way to give even a spartan bath spa appeal. For finishing touches, throw in white towels in thirsty textured weaves, a tub tray stocked with scented soap, soft candlelight, and a dressing chair to hold other essentials.

Treat your writing desk to the sensual pleasures of handmade paper. An embossed wallcovering, good-to-the-hand writing papers, and a deep frame featuring papyrus keep this monochromatic scheme filled with soothing experiences.

The Scandinavians have the right idea. In a land where the winter sun seldom shines, white is revered for its ability to reflect and enhance the waning light. Here, white walls come in to comfort a room of rest.

Surround a bedside with a folding screen to give it warmth and intimacy. A small can light tucked behind this rice-paper screen bathes the room in a golden glow. You can build a rice-paper screen from import-store rice-paper shades and lumber-store stock. If you're not a craftsperson or want a quicker decorating result, look for free-standing floor screens in mail-order catalogs and home furnishings stores. They'll range from wood, bamboo, and wicker to iron and fabric structures. Sometimes you can find empty screen frames in antiques shops and stretch your own fabric over the rails. To locate can lights for that uplight glow behind the screen, ask for help in lighting stores or in the lighting sections of home improvement centers and large hardware stores.

To make the most of all-white interiors, take out the slickness and banish the chill with textural, translucent fabrics. Hang bed curtains from rods attached to the ceiling. They'll wrap the headboard with protective airs, cutting off the cold drafts of night. Vintage-style organdy and eyelet bedcoverings for winter duvets keep the blanketed bed looking light and inviting. Purchase a cotton duvet that can be whisked off for easy cleaning.

entertain

guests

1
snow bowl

Light a cold-weather

party with a host of

candles. To make this

sparkling bowl of lights,

purchase a dozen

slender tapers. Place a

block of floral foam in

the bottom of a silver

bowl. Insert the candles

into the foam, fill the

bowl with sugar to hide

the foam, and allow the

wax to drip into the

"snow."

2 votive chandelier

Spray-paint a secondhand chandelier with white paint after removing all of the wiring. Use purchased glass pendants or assemble your own from crafts store beads and wire and hang one from each arm. Place glass votive candleholders in the chandelier cups. Drop in votive candles, or use purchased gel wax candles. (Keep the flames well away from fabric or flammable material.)

3 it's my party

Cover a table with richly textured fabric. For the centerpiece, decorate a cake stand with inexpensive strands of colored beads and a fanciful cake set on top. Roll napkins into "roses" by first folding them in narrow strips. Then make the flower centers by wrapping one end of each strip around your forefinger. Wrap the rest of each strip tightly around the center and place the roses in sherbet cups to keep their shapes. Tuck tinsel-topped skewers into the roses. Scatter more beads on the tabletop, light the votive candles, and call it a party.

4 ribbon roses

Wind the end of a yard-long length of 1½-inch-wide voile ribbon around a pencil five times for the center. For petals, hold the flower center in one hand while you loop, twist, and pinch the ribbon to the bottom of the bud. At intervals, secure a few petals with thread. Add florist's leaves to the back of the rose.

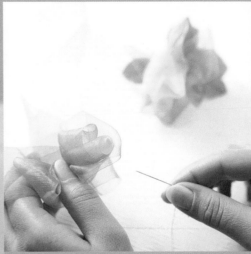

party 5 on ice

For a frozen champagne bucket spiked with rose petals, start by partially filling a plastic bowl with ice cubes and fresh petals. Insert a plastic liter bottle half-filled with salt water to create a cavity for the champagne bottle. Fill the rest of the bowl with water and freeze it. To dislodge the ice bucket, immerse the plastic bowl in hot water and fill the liter bottle with hot water. Set the champagne bottle in the opening made for it and place the ice bowl in a silver bowl of similar size on a buffet table.

night lights

Trade a standard chandelier for pools of light to add low-key drama to a dining room. To set the mood, hang an adjustable pendant lamp that can be raised for overall lighting and lowered for cozier gatherings. Look for a fixture that softens and diffuses the light so that diners aren't blinded. Installing a dimmer allows more flexibility.

Strip lighting, like the low-profile fixtures on the sides of this china cupboard, makes dishes and glassware shine. Concealed strips, which plug in for easy installation, also could be mounted beneath shelves and on top of a cupboard.

Candlelight raises a room's emotional temperature. Spark things up with votive candles on the table and sideboard—even around a pendant lamp (place them carefully).

year-round
furniture
arranging

Rearranging your furniture is an easy way to give a room a fresh new look. If you enjoy the vitality that making changes with the seasons can bring to your home, study the following pages for ideas and inspiration. You'll find illustrations showing how to arrange furniture in typical room configurations to make the most of what each season has to offer. If you're shopping for new furniture, check out the suggestions for the 12 best pieces that provide the highest level of flexibility and usefulness.

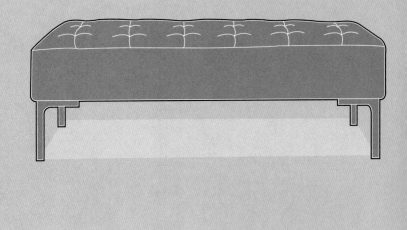

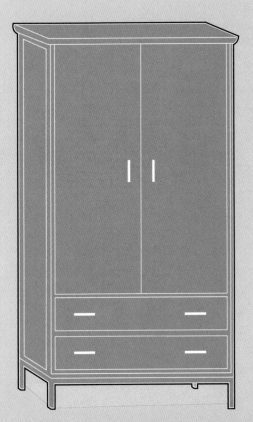

tunnel room one

Dual-purpose living rooms and family rooms with single entrances often appear so long and narrow that they're labeled "tunnel rooms." To give a wide and spacious look to a room with tunnel vision, break up the length of the room with blocks of furniture. Place chairs and tables at angles, set a sofa crosswise in the room, and use tables with curves for ease in walking around. The arrangements in this staircased room gently direct traffic around the conversation area rather than through it. For summer, the arrangement is open for a free-spirited feel, while the winter arrangement adds furniture for indoor activities.

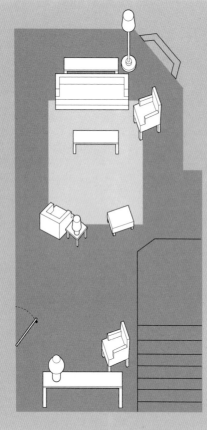

spring/summer

A sofa is placed across the room at the back of this open and relaxed seating arrangement as a focal point for the room and an anchor for conversation. Traffic from the entry at the left of the room flows easily up the stairs or into the end-of-the-room group. The long entry table and chair maintain the look of a foyer year-round.

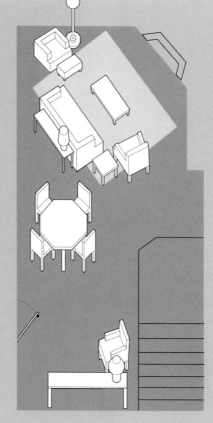

autumn/winter

For cool months the seating group gathers around the fireplace. The area rug runs parallel to the hearth, and the sofa anchors the back of the conversation area as it faces the fire. The remaining chairs and tables follow suit, forming a U-shape arrangement. This tightens the summer look and creates space for a game table and chairs, adding more indoor function to the room for the season.

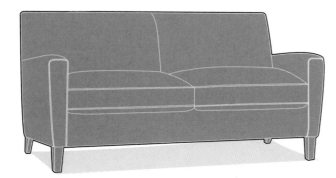

two-seat sofa

For a number of reasons, the two-seat sofa is a choice piece of furniture for flexible room arranging. First, it provides comfortable seating, a basic necessity in any home. Second, it's lightweight and easily moved about. Third, it's a better choice than the long sofa that seats people in a row like birds on a fence. Rarely does the long sofa work better than the short one.

tunnel room two

A long, narrow room with furniture lined up along the walls has all the charm of a waiting room. This common furniture arrangement exaggerates the length of a tunnel room and keeps its occupants at a distance. The solution? Divide the length of the room into two or three intimate areas that ease conversation and add function to the space. These furniture arrangements turn this large, formal living room into a treasury of cozy seating groups that avoid the need to shout across a room. In addition, they offer semiannual changes to keep the room fresh and geared for gathering in any season.

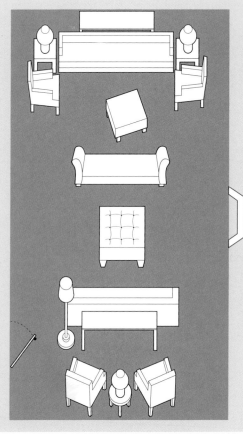

spring/summer

An open arrangement for summer's airy style is created by placing two sofas across the room from each other. In the center, a settee conveniently faces either sofa for conversation; ottomans work as coffee tables on both sides of it. At the end of the room near the entrance, two armchairs invite an intimate talk across from the sofa/entry table.

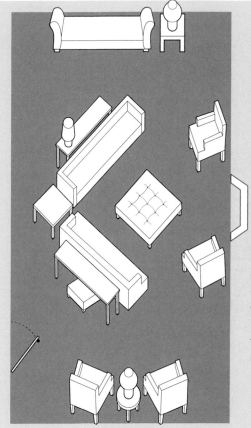

autumn/winter

Come fall, the two main sofas move to the center of the room in a right-angle arrangement in front of the fire. The two sofa tables move with them for lighting and easy behind-the-sofa service. The backless sofa moves to the end wall by the windows for a well-lit reading corner and scenic winter naps. One of the square tables fills out the right-angle arrangement at the corner and the other one is placed at the end of the backless sofa. The two small armchairs remain near the entrance under a mirror or painting.

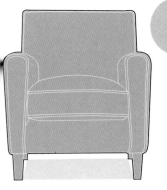

armchair

The armchair is a true companion to the sofa, working in partnership to form a complete seating group. One chair and a short sofa are fine in a small room, but you may prefer two armchairs in a larger room. Place them as a pair opposite a sofa, as a pair by themselves in a room, or in a U-shape arrangement with each chair at a right angle to the ends of a sofa.

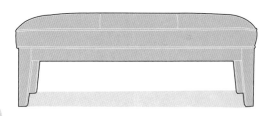

backless bench

Nothing provides flexible, movable seating like a bench. Use it in a hall, at the end of a bed, as an ottoman, or at an extended holiday table for extra seating. To use it as a crossover piece in a long seating group, place it in the center of the group where it can provide seating from either side.

open plan one

Arranging furniture in an open plan can be difficult to accomplish in a single try but easy if you're willing to arrange and rearrange pieces until the right solution falls into place. Sometimes planning ideas on paper with a room-arranging kit or a grid and furniture pieces you devise yourself eases experimentation and avoids the physical difficulties of moving heavy furniture around. First, list the ways you use the room. Then eliminate furniture pieces that don't work and plan for new ones that will serve you better.

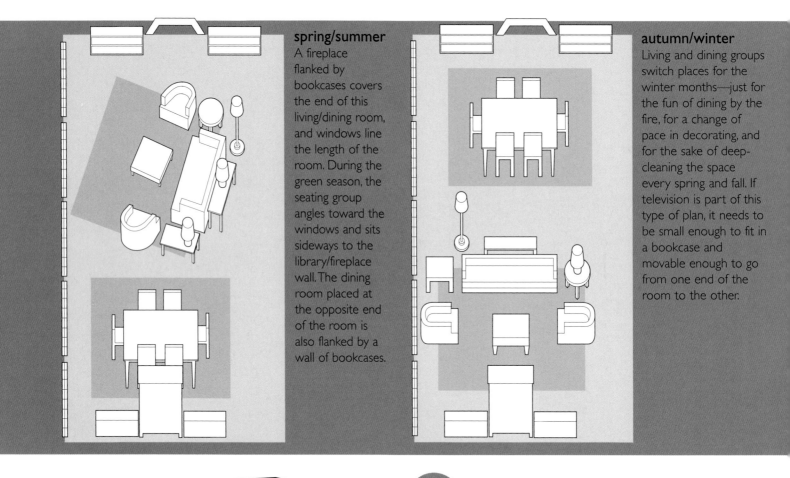

spring/summer
A fireplace flanked by bookcases covers the end of this living/dining room, and windows line the length of the room. During the green season, the seating group angles toward the windows and sits sideways to the library/fireplace wall. The dining room placed at the opposite end of the room is also flanked by a wall of bookcases.

autumn/winter
Living and dining groups switch places for the winter months—just for the fun of dining by the fire, for a change of pace in decorating, and for the sake of deep-cleaning the space every spring and fall. If television is part of this type of plan, it needs to be small enough to fit in a bookcase and movable enough to go from one end of the room to the other.

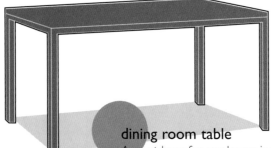

dining room table
A must-have for any home is a smooth, inviting surface for dining. For the most flexibility, choose a table that is simple in design and lightweight in material so that moving it is easy. If your dining room has space, a table with extra leaves is a practical choice.

dining room chairs
Without chairs, the dining table doesn't function; they're high on the list for furniture-arranging flexibility. Avoid chairs that are clumsy looking and too heavy to move easily. Choose chairs that allow at least 6 inches of space between them when placed at the table.

open plan two

An open plan, common in suburban homes, may be blessed with an architectural niche—a windowed banquette for dining that offers a panoramic view of the ever-changing landscape. While such built-ins keep the dining room furniture at the same end of the room year-round, subtle rearranging of furniture pieces within each living/dining group alters the functions of each area in ways that are appropriate to the season.

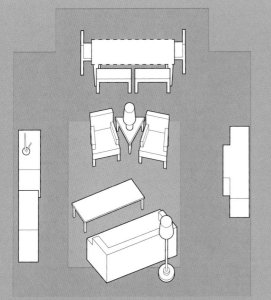

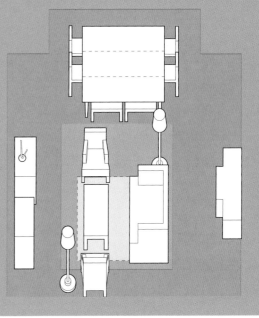

autumn/winter

The harvest table expands for family dinners and holiday celebrations when the outdoor table closes down for the season. Backless benches along the long side of the table work two ways—sometimes they seat dinner guests; at other times they turn about to face the living room area. For winter months, the living room seating is squared up for a more formal, orderly look. The breakfront opposite the television wall remains in place all year and works as a welcoming piece as well as a storage unit near the front entrance.

spring/summer

The dining niche is slimmed down when the days for eating outdoors take pressure off the banquette. The leaves of the harvest table drop for most of the season, allowing for freer traffic flow in and out of the house. The seating group changes to a diagonal arrangement, implying more activity and movement within the room.

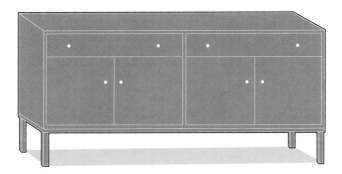

buffet

A china cupboard or dining-room storage comes in many forms, but for seasonal changes, low, lightweight pieces are best. While conventional highboys and china closets make excellent focal-point statements in a room, long, horizontal pieces provide more surface for buffet-style food service and flexibility in room arranging.

corridor room one

A corridor room is one that connects the front entry with the rest of the house. In the illustration, the front door is at the lower left corner. The entry to the kitchen is directly across from the front door, and a hall to the bedrooms lies diagonally opposite the entry. Directing foot traffic through the room is the main function of furniture arranging. Make sure traffic flows around—not through—the conversation area. Group chairs and sofas, guiding people to walk behind and beside the area, not between the seating pieces.

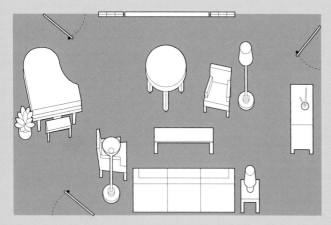

autumn/winter

In winter, the sofa turns away from frosty windows to a focal-point wall of art. The rearrangement changes the focus of the space and brings the piano into the conversation area during the months when family and friends want most to gather around it. The round table changes from an occasional dining surface to a library stockpiled with winter reading.

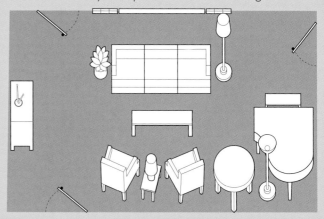

spring/summer

In summer, this sectional seating group faces the windows on the opposite wall to take advantage of the light and green, grassy view. A round tea table stands near the window at a distance far enough to keep the traffic flowing around the conversation area. The table invites the armchairs to move to the table near the window for an occasional meal.

wicker chair

An armchair made of lightweight wicker can be moved easily from room to room and function in a variety of ways. Like an upholstered armchair, it can pair with another in a complete and intimate seating group or join a seating group as an extra (and distinctive) piece. It can be a singular piece in a hall or bedroom. It can also provide variety at the dining room table by serving at the head and end of the table when the table is extended and added seating is needed.

corridor room two

In many tract homes, the front entrance opens into a living/dining corridor room. In the illustrations *below*, the front door is at the lower right; the kitchen door is on the opposite wall. At the upper left corner, a door leads to the bedroom wing. Windows span the front entrance wall, making the wall opposite it the only logical place for a large television and bookcases. For the winter months, the entertainment wall is the focal point; in summer, the arrangement focuses on the windowed wall.

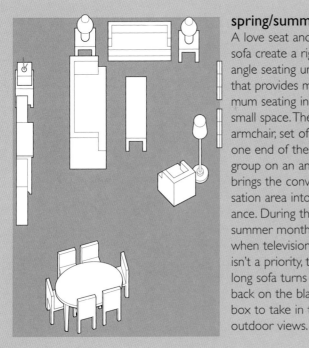

spring/summer

A love seat and sofa create a right-angle seating unit that provides maximum seating in a small space. The armchair, set off at one end of the group on an angle, brings the conversation area into balance. During the summer months, when television isn't a priority, the long sofa turns its back on the black box to take in the outdoor views.

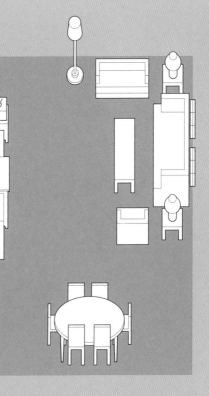

autumn/winter

Here the seating group squares up in a tighter, closer conversation group that turns around to face the television set. A fireplace offers a logical winter focal point as well, and in many homes, the fireplace is part of a built-in bookcase and entertainment center.

armoire

While a large armoire can be difficult to move once set in place, it can serve many purposes. In a bedroom, it's an extra closet; in a work space, an office in a box. In the living room, it's a focal-point cornerstone piece (usually an entertainment center) around which all other furniture gathers.

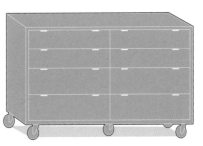

rolling storage

Modern life demands flexibility, and a storage piece on wheels is one of the better ways to supply it. Like the Hollywood bed frame, a rolling cart can move from position to position and be locked down when a desirable placement is found.

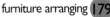

L-shape room one

Homes built in the 1970s often sport an open plan, with an L-shape configuration that wraps around the kitchen. The short end of the L is generally labeled the dining area and opens directly into the kitchen. The entrance to this L-shape plan is on the upper right corner of the living area and exits onto a deck opposite the front door. While the open space is a plus, it can look too busy if numerous small-scale pieces fill the room. Keep furniture pieces at a minimum for a peaceful, relaxed look and keep the traffic path open.

spring/summer

For active, outdoor months when traffic flows through the house at a rapid pace, place the conversation seating group on an angle for easy access from the deck. Furniture placed diagonally adds casual spirit and movement to an interior space.

autumn/winter

Formalize for the winter months, squaring up the seating group and directing it toward the fireplace or entertainment wall. Less clutter and an orderly arrangement allow the dining room table to be extended for the holidays.

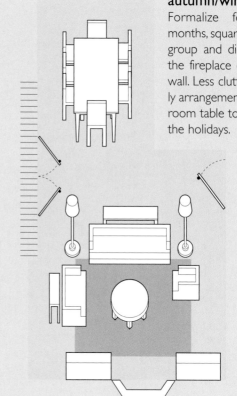

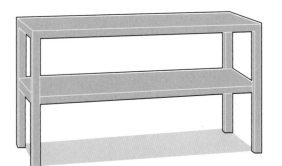

console table

A long, narrow table serves in a front hall as a welcoming surface or as a handy storage piece at the head of a bed. Most often, it's useful for defining a seating group when it's placed behind main seating pieces. Behind a sofa, the console table holds over-the-shoulder lighting and keeps sofa-side items within easy reach. It also works as an easy-to-access dining room storage unit and buffet surface.

L-shape room two

A wide, French-door entrance at the upper left corner of this L-shape plan requires a wide hall in front of it for traffic flow. While the architecture of the space is attractive, the chance for seasonal furniture rearranging is limited. The short end of the L logically becomes the dining room because of its proximity to the kitchen, and barstools invite casual dining on the other edge of the large kitchen. Flexible sectional seating is chosen for ease of rearranging.

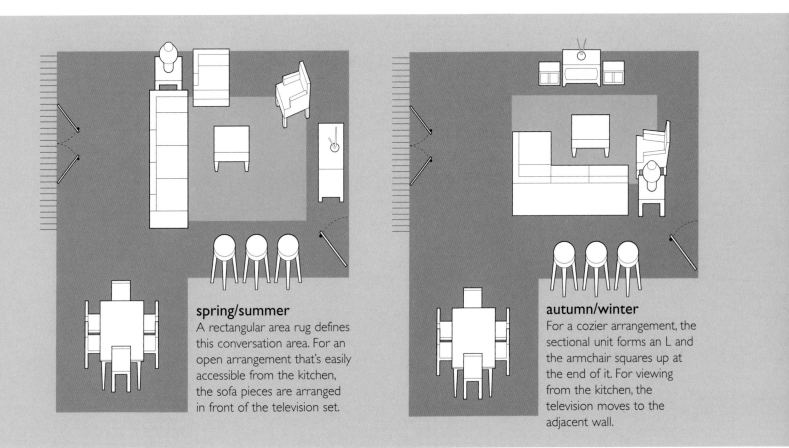

spring/summer
A rectangular area rug defines this conversation area. For an open arrangement that's easily accessible from the kitchen, the sofa pieces are arranged in front of the television set.

autumn/winter
For a cozier arrangement, the sectional unit forms an L and the armchair squares up at the end of it. For viewing from the kitchen, the television moves to the adjacent wall.

ottoman
Choose a large, upholstered ottoman instead of a heavy coffee table for a seating group; it's easier to move about and more inviting. Because a coffee table often gets the feet-on-top treatment anyway, make it a guilt-free experience by providing the gang with a soft surface for leaning back. When it's time for food service, turn the ottoman into a coffee table by setting a large tray on top of the upholstery so food won't be associated with feet.

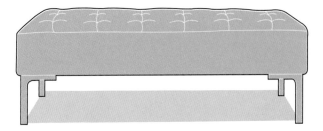

master suite

The ultimate goal of arranging and rearranging a master suite is to give it a getaway feel. Keep floor spaces as open as possible for a relaxed look, and gather a variety of furniture pieces that extend the use of the room beyond merely getting rest. The plans shown here are typical of new construction, in which builders include architectural bump-outs in master suites. For decorating ideas, borrow elements you enjoyed in your favorite hotel rooms from vacation trips. They can help you capture the experience of a great escape.

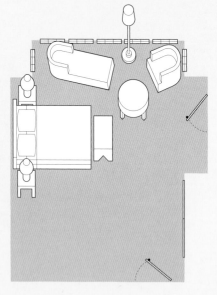

spring/summer

In spring and summer, the bed moves close to the windowed niche, leaving extra floor space for easy access to the door, bath, and walk-in closets. When the headboard is placed on the wall near the window, the treetops and sounds of nature are brought closer.

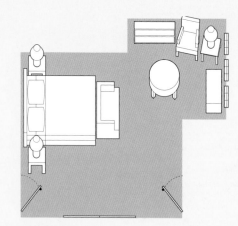

spring/summer

In this bedroom with a corner bump-out, the bed faces the windows in summer. The love seat at the end of the bed also takes advantage of the view. A large, round ottoman suggests a spacious and luxurious space for conversation at the end of a long day.

autumn/winter

The head of the bed is placed on the short wall next to the door, bath, and closets. While this placement doesn't allow the sleeper to view anyone entering the room, the bed is positioned in the warmest place of the room and opposite to the windows full of wintry views.

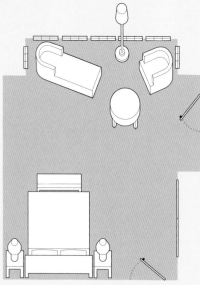

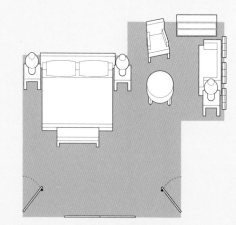

autumn/winter

The bed turns to face inward for the winter while the seating pieces cluster cozily in the bump-out. The proximity of the furniture to the windowed corner may not appeal to homeowners in northern parts of the country, but in the south, the rearrangement is a refreshing change.

hints and tips

Use your brain and save your back. Moving furniture is hard work, so have a plan before you begin. Use a room-arranging kit to do a layout to scale. Or do the same thing in full scale: Cut cardboard templates for each piece of furniture, move the existing furniture out, and move the cutouts around the room until you get a layout that works. At the same time, consider light sources; check to see whether outlets are where you need them.

Avoid whole room sets of furniture. You'll be stuck with their stiff, inflexible arrangements. Acquire furniture one piece at a time, keeping it compatible in style with other furnishings in the house. Then you can move pieces from room to room as your decorating whims change. Also, before arranging, take stock of what you have and how you'll be using spaces to gain a better understanding of what you need.

Choose one or two significant pieces for each room to avoid the dollhouse look of too many small pieces. These pieces, along with any strong architectural features like a fireplace, help to anchor a room and give it substance.

Remember the focal point. The goal of any room arrangement is to create a simple grouping of furniture pieces that work toward the room's purposes—dining, sleeping, working, eating, and relaxing. Each room should have an architectural feature or dominant piece of furniture that creates the main focus or visual reference point around which all other pieces are oriented.

Direct traffic. Pay attention to how people move through the room—and how you want them to move through the room. Eliminate traffic blockades by getting rid of extra furniture pieces that stand in the way. Create an easy path through the room without directing traffic through a conversation group. Allow a path about 3 feet wide where you want traffic to flow.

Make islands of comfort. Tighten furniture into islands that serve well-defined purposes and carve out areas within a room. For example, place a console table behind a sofa that sits at a right angle to a doorway, creating a back "wall" for a conversation group. An area rug also defines a furniture island. Or place a seating piece at the foot of the bed for extended bedroom comfort.

canopy bed

While a bed with a canopy is not a necessity, it's nice. If you choose one, you can dress it in a wardrobe of bed linens and blankets that change with the seasons. During summer months, enjoy it in a stripped-down state with its bare-bones structure showing you a cool, lean look. In winter, see the canopy as a protective structure, a room-within-a-room where you can snuggle inside bed curtains and sleep luxuriously beneath deep, warm comforters.

buying guide and credits

INTRODUCTION

pages 4–7: Manilla wicker chair, Gideon half-round console table, Amery nesting tables: Room & Board, Home Furnishings 800/486-6554; roomandboard.com

Glass urn: Pier 1 Imports; for a local retail store, call 800/447-4371.

design, REBECCA JERDEE; photos, KIM CORNELISON

SPRING

pages 8–9: All items: antique, discontinued, or a personal belonging

produced by SUNDIE RUPPERT; photos, KIM CORNELISON

pages 10–11: White wing chairs: Ralph Lauren Home Collection, 212/642-8700. **Plates, candlestick, ironstone bowls, pitcher:** antique

pages 12–13: Pink luster dishes: Bountiful, 1335 Abbot Kinney Blvd., Venice, CA 90291

pages 16–17: Porch rocking chairs: Lexington Furniture Industries, 800/539-4636

pages 10–17: produced by MARY ANNE THOMSON; photos, ALISE O'BRIEN. Special thanks to Kim and Joseph Morrow, St. Louis, Missouri, for sharing their home.

pages 18–19: All items: antique, discontinued, or a personal belonging

page 18: design, MARTHA FOSS; photos, JAMIE HADLEY

page 19: top, design, EMILIE BARNES; photo, MARK LOHMAN; bottom, produced by ESTELLE BOND GURALNIK; photo, ERIC ROTH

page 20: Bedside lamp, wooden tray: similar styles available at The Gate House, 888/446-6269; gatehousela.com

page 20: design, ANN PORTER; produced by ROBIN TUCKER; photo, JON JENSEN

pages 24–25: photo, LANGDON CLAY

page 26: Duvet cover: IRKE from IKEA, 800/434-4532. **Cable curtain rod:** FREKVENS from IKEA, 800/434-4532

All other items: antique, discontinued, or a personal belonging

interior design, REBECCA JERDEE; photo, KING AU

page 27: Floor lamp, sofa, pillows: similar styles available at The Gate House, 888/446-6269; gatehousela.com

interior design, ANN PORTER; produced by ROBIN TUCKER; photo, JON JENSEN

page 28: Wall-hung table: AKKA from IKEA, 800/434-4532. **Settee cushion fabric:** "Mistral" (Canary) from Calico Corners, 800/777-9933 **Curtain fabric:** "La Poeme" (Canary) from Calico Corners, 800/777-9933

page 28: design, REBECCA JERDEE; photo, KING AU

page 29: design, REBECCA JERDEE; photo, WILLIAM STITES

pages 30–31: design, PEGGY JOHNSTON; photo, KIM CORNELISON

page 32: To order **seashells** like those shown in the photographs, check seashells.com or visit your local crafts store.

pages 34–39: Cotton voile fabrics: similar styles available at fabric stores

designs, REBECCA JERDEE; photos, KIM CORNELISON

pages 40–41: Beaded-board planks: available at home improvement centers

pages 42–43: Pilaster moldings, decorative blocks, dentil crown

molding: similar styles available at home improvement centers

pages 40–43: designs, DAVE UNDERWOOD; photos, KIM CORNELISON

pages 44–45: Victorian bed: Model 390 (Pine), Woodmaster of San Antonio, uffos.com; 877/583-9742. **Hardwood accents on bed:** 307 (headboard), 303 (footboard), 311 (posts) from House of Fara, 800/334-1732 **Paint on bed:** SW1523 (Huckleberry), SW1004 (Pure White), Sherwin-Williams; for a store near you, call 800/474-3794. **Bedding, bedspread, shams, pillows:** similar styles available from The Company Store, 800/285-3696

pages 44–45: design, GINA HARRELL; photos, LARK SMOTHERMON

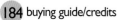

pages 46–49: **Truman sofa, Manilla wicker chair, Truman chair and ottoman, Lansing coffee table:** Room & Board, Home Furnishings, 800/486-6554; roomandboard.com
Screen, pillows, throw, baskets: similar styles available from Pier 1 Imports, for a local retail store, call 800/447-4371.
Area rugs: IKEA, 800/434-4532. **Sofa and chair slipcovers:** L. L. Bean, Inc., Freeport, ME 04033, 800/809-7057

interior design, REBECCA JERDEE; photos, KIM CORNELISON

SUMMER

pages 50–51: **All items:** antique, discontinued, or a personal belonging

produced by SUNDIE RUPPERT; photos, KIM CORNELISON

pages 52–55: **Wicker furniture:** Lloyd/Flanders Industries, Inc., P. O. Box 550, Menominee, MI 49858, 800/526-9894

page 59: **Adirondack chairs:** L. L. Bean, Inc., Freeport, ME 04033, 800/809-7057

pages 52–59: interior design, SANDY TOFANELLI-GORDON; produced by ANDREA CAUGHEY; photos, ED GOHLICH
page 60: photo, WILLIAM STITES
page 61: photo, KING AU

pages 62–63: **All items:** antique, discontinued, or a personal belonging

page 62: interior design, BARBIE ROSTAD; photo, MICHAEL JENSEN
page 63: photo, WILLIAM STITES

page 65: **Chandelier:** antique

design, REBECCA JERDEE; photo, KIM CORNELISON

pages 66–67: **All items:** antique, discontinued, or a personal belonging

interior design, BARBARA RANDLE; produced by DEBRA HASTINGS; photos, D. RANDOLPH FOULDS

pages 68–69: **Bistro chairs:** Palacek, 800/274-7730

pages 70–71: **Cable hardware:** similar styles available from IKEA, 800/434-4532

pages 80–81: **Paper lanterns:** IKEA, 800/434-4532
Bamboo poles: Pier 1 Imports, for a local retail store, call 800/447-4371.

pages 68–73: interior designs, REBECCA JERDEE; photos, KING AU
pages 74–75: design, CATHERINE KRAMER; photos, WILLIAM HOPKINS
pages 76–83: designs, REBECCA JERDEE; photos, KIM CORNELISON

pages 82–83: **Interior paints:** SW1701 (Mariposa), SW1820 (China Aster), Sherwin-Williams; for a store near you, call 800/474-3794.

pages 84–85: photos, KING AU

pages 86–87: **Glazing paint:** Glaze Vernis (Pompeii Red) 50308, Glaze Vernis (White) 53006, **sponging mitt** 30105, **decorator blocks** 53226, **wall glaze** 53551 (Neutral), Plaid Enterprises, 800/842-4197

design, PAULA HAMILTON, MARY MULCAHY; photos, JAMES YOCHUM

pages 88–91: **Portica dining table, Venice dining chairs:** Room & Board, Home Furnishings, 800/486-6554; roomandboard.com
Fireplace, windows: antique
White flower bucket, lantern hooks: Restoration Hardware
Green vases, white tablecloth: IKEA, 800/434-4532
Frosted glass urns, bucket: Nautica, available in fine department stores
Woven throw: JCPenney Home Collection, 800/222-6161

interior designs, REBECCA JERDEE; photos, KIM CORNELISON

AUTUMN

pages 92–93: All items: antique, discontinued, or a personal belonging
produced by SUNDIE RUPPERT; photos, KIM CORNELISON

pages 94–101: All items: antique; for similar pieces:

Joanne Boardman Antiques
522 Joanne Ln.
De Kalb, IL 60115
815/756-9359 (by appointment)

Marie Plummer and John Philbrick
68 E. Main St.
Yarmouth, ME 04096
(by appointment)

Mountain Crest Antiques
45 Lawrence Plain Rd.,
Rte. 47
S. Hadley, MA 01035
413/586-0352 (by appointment)

Stephen Douglas Antiques
P. O. Box 27
Rockingham, VT 05101
802/463-4296 (by appointment)

pages 94–101: interior design, SHARON MATSON; produced by GARY THOMSON; photos, WILLIAM STITES

pages 102–107: All items: antique, discontinued, or a personal belonging
pages 102–105: produced by BARBARA MUNDALL; photos, JON JENSEN
page 106: top photo, JON JENSEN; produced by BARBARA MUNDALL; bottom photo, KING AU
page 107: produced by ESTELLE BOND GURALNIK; photo, WILLIAM STITES
pages 109–111: photo, KING AU

pages 112–113: All items: antique, discontinued, or a personal belonging
page 112: produced by CATHERINE KRAMER; photos, WILLIAM HOPKINS
pages 114–115: interior design, REBECCA JERDEE; photo, KING AU

pages 116–117: Paint for color combing: Laura Ashley 702 (base coat), 704 Deep Cowslip (top coat), Laura Ashley paints, available at Lowe's, Inc., 800/445-6937; lowes.com
design, PATRICIA MOHR KRAMER; photos, HOPKINS ASSOCIATES

pages 118–119: Paint for leaf stenciling: SW1402 Pear Tint (background), SW1440 Pesto (leaves), Sherwin-Williams, for a store near you, call 800/474-3794.
design, PATRICIA MOHR KRAMER; photos, HOPKINS ASSOCIATES

pages 120–125: All items: antique, discontinued, or a personal belonging
pages 120–123: designs, REBECCA JERDEE; photos, KIM CORNELISON
page 124: photo, KING AU
page 125: photos, JAMIE HADLEY
page 126: design, WADE SCHERRER; photo, KING AU

page 127: Silk fabric: "Mysore" (Gold), Calico Corners, Walnut Road Business Park, 203 Gale Ln., Kennett Square, PA 19348; 800/213-6366 **Braided cord:** twisted acetate ³⁄₁₆-inch cord #8641 (color C12), Conso Products, P. O. Box 326, Union, SC 29379; 800/845-2431. **Bamboo rod** (Tortoise Shell), **bracket** (Grace in French Oak), **ball finial** (Acanthus in French Oak), Antique Drapery Rod Co., 140 Glass St., Dallas, TX 75207; 214/653-1733 (available only through design professionals). **Wallpaper:** Ornamenta (from the Architecture by Raymond Waites collection #545170), Gramercy, 800/332-3384

page 128: Tablecloths: "Peony" (Slate), Cornell Trading, Inc., 802/879-5100; aprilcornell.com
Hardware: Wrought Iron Collection, Graber by Springs Window Fashions, Customer Service Center, Box 500, Rte. 405, Montgomery, PA 17752; 800/221-6352
Bed: Eddie Bauer Home, 800/426-8020; eddiebauer.com
Sheets: Laura Ashley, 800/367-2000
pages 127–128: design, HEIDI KLUZAK; photos, HOPKINS ASSOCIATES
page 129: photo, KING AU

pages 130–133: Taylor bed, Amery nesting tables, under-the-bed storage drawer: Room & Board, Home Furnishings 800/486-6554; roomandboard.com
White throw, autumn quilt, sheets, pillowcases: similar styles available from JCPenney Home Collection, 800/222-6161
Lamp: IKEA, 800/434-4532
interior designs, REBECCA JERDEE; photos, KIM CORNELISON

WINTER

pages 134–135: **All items:** antique, discontinued, or a personal belonging
produced by REBECCA JERDEE; photos, KIM CORNELISON

pages 136–143:
Accessories on commode and mantel, pedestal cocktail table, floor lamps: made from 19th-century French torchères. **Bed linens:** Ann Gish, Inc., Newbury Park, CA, 805/498-4447
Architectural capitals as bedside tables: Mimi Williams Interiors, Atlanta, 404/885-1530
pages 136–141, 143: interior design, MIMI WILLIAMS; architectural design, DUANE STONE; produced by LISA MOWRY; photos, RICK TAYLOR
page 142: photo, JEFF McNAMARA

pages 144–149: **All items:** antique, discontinued, or a personal belonging

page 144: photo, ERIC ROTH
page 145: design, PEGGY JOHNSTON; photo, KIM CORNELISON
pages 146–147: produced by MARY ANNE THOMSON; photos, ALISE O'BRIEN
pages 148–149: designs, PEGGY JOHNSTON; photos, KIM CORNELISON

pages 150–151: **Sofas:** Drexel Heritage Furnishings, Inc., 101 N. Main St., Drexel, NC 28619; visit the website at www.drexelheritage.com to find a store near you.
produced by MARY ANNE THOMSON; photo, ALISE O'BRIEN

page 155: **Pillow shams:** similar styles available at Target Stores. **Velvet pillow, urn:** similar styles available at Pier 1 Imports, for a local retail store, call 800/447-4371.
pages 152–155: photos, KING AU

pages 156–157: **All items:** antique, discontinued, or a personal belonging
design, PAULA HAMILTON, MARY MULCAHY; photos, KIM CORNELISON

pages 158–159: **Black and white prints:** IKEA, 800/434-4532
designs, AMY UNDERWOOD; photos, KIM CORNELISON

pages 160–161: **Fabric dyes:** Kelly Green, Teal, RIT, available in grocery stores
designs, AMY UNDERWOOD photos, KIM CORNELISON

pages 162–163: **All items:** antique, discontinued, or a personal belonging
page 162: photo, KIM CORNELISON

pages 164–165: **Textured fabrics:** similar items available through Lands' End Catalog, 800/345-3696
pages 163–165: photos, SUSAN GILMORE

pages 166–167: **Place setting:** Rosenthal Line "Classic Rose," discontinued
page 166: design, MICHELLE MICHAEL; photo, MICHAEL GARLAND
page 167: designs, PEGGY JOHNSTON; photos, KIM CORNELISON

pages 168–170: **All items:** antique, discontinued, or a personal belonging
page 168: photos, KIM CORNELISON
page 169: design, MICHELLE MICHAEL; photo, MICHAEL GARLAND

page 171: **Strip lighting:** Juno Lighting, 847/827-9880
All other items: antique, discontinued, or a personal belonging
pages 170–171: interior design, REBECCA JERDEE; photo, SUSAN GILMORE

FURNITURE ARRANGING

pages 172–183: illustrations, LORI GOULD

general index

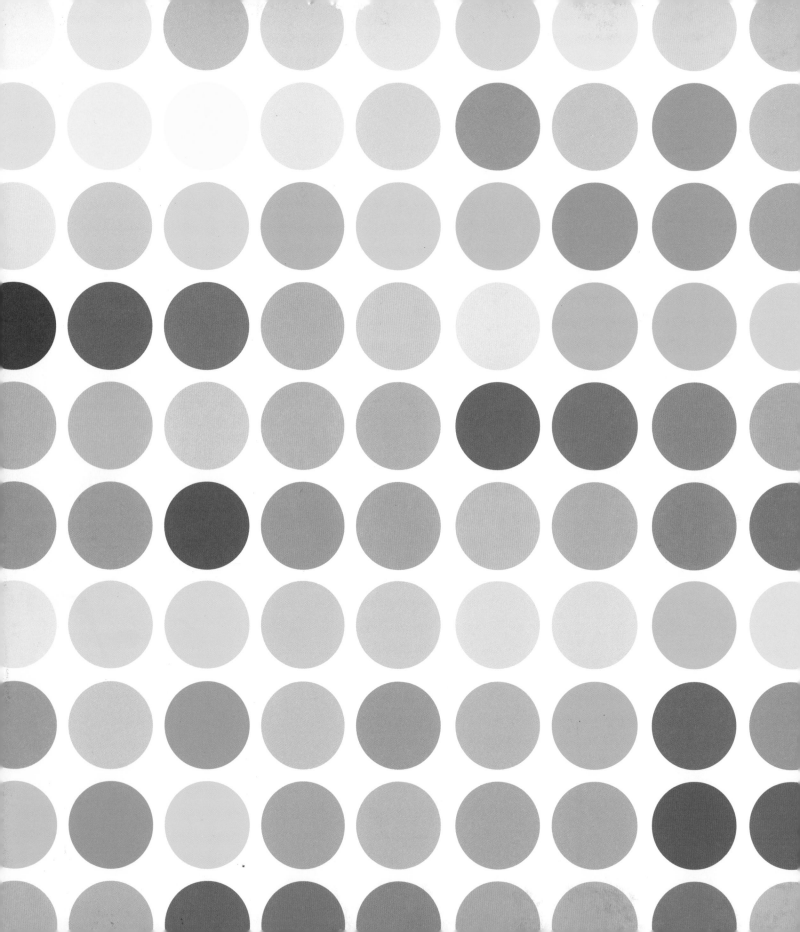